Contents

C000260299

Collins

KEY STAGE 3

HISTORY

BOOK 3: TWENTIETH CENTURY

F WILKINSON, DAVE MARTIN, JO PEARSON, SUE WILKINSON, ANDREW WRENN

Published by Collins Education
An imprint of HarperCollins Publishers
The News Building
1 London Bridge Street,
London
SE1 9GF

Browse the complete Collins catalogue at
www.collinseducation.com

10 9 8 7 6 5

ISBN 978 0 00 7345762

British Library Cataloguing in Publication Data.
A Catalogue record for this publication is available from the British Library.

Commissioning Editors: Charlie Evans, Lucy McLoughlin
Project Editor: Tim Satterthwaite
Concept Design: EMC Design
Page Design: Ken Vail Graphic Design
Illustrations by Ken Vail Graphic Design
Cover Design by Joerg Hartmannsgruber, White-Card
Production: Simon Moore
Printed and bound by CPI Group (UK) Ltd, Croydon, CR0 4YY

With particular thanks to Natalie Andrews.

Unit 5   Life in Britain in the twentieth century   170

The twentieth century
Part 1: The age of total war

South African War (1899–1902)

World War One (1914–1918) Known as 'the war to end all wars' (pages 12–49)

Chinese-Japanese War (1937–1945) (pages 84-85)

World War Two (1939–1945) The first 'total war' (pages 92–130)

Vietnam War (1945–1975) War between the USSR-supported North Vietnam, and the USA-supported South Vietnam (pages 138–139)

Cold War (1946–1989) A 'war' about two different *ideologies*: capitalism and communism (pages 132–149)

Arab-Israeli Conflict (1948 to present) (pages 152–155)

Korean War (1950–1953) War between the USSR-supported North Korea and the USA-supported South Korea (pages 146–147)

Afghan War (1979–1988) Brezhnev sent Soviet troops to help the Afghan government fight guerrillas (pages 158–159)

Bosnia (1992–1995) This conflict started following the break-up of Yugoslavia (pages 154–155)

Rwanda (1994) About one million people were killed in acts of *genocide*

'War on Terror' (2001 to present) A global 'war' against international terrorism (pages 152–161)

Ethnic cleansing: the violent removal of one ethnic group by another ethnic group

Although there have been no 'world wars' since 1945, there has never been a year of peace. A range of ideas – including nationalism, religion and *ethnic cleansing* – have been used as reasons for wars, in which millions of people have died. Let's explore some of these conflicts, and try to think about their impact.

During the 20th century there were two major wars that between them caused the deaths of nearly 100 million people. New technologies made killing easy, changing the face of war forever. Machine guns, poison gas and tanks were introduced in World War One. Later scientists developed atom bombs, which were dropped on Hiroshima and Nagasaki in Japan in 1945, in the final months of World War Two. Certain ideas also made people more willing to kill each other. For example, the German Nazis' desire to create a 'master race' led to the Holocaust, an attempt to wipe out the Jewish people.

Now it's your turn

1 Draw a timeline showing the main wars of the 20th century.
2 Can you think of any other 20th century wars? Make a list of these with your classmates, and then try to find out three pieces of information about each of them. Add this information to your timeline.
3 Can you sort these conflicts into groups? What do some of them have in common? How are they different from each other?

Extension work

1 Which conflict do you think has had the biggest impact on the 20th century? Why?
2 What does your timeline tell you about the 20th century?

Check your progress

I can talk about some wars in 20th century.
I can explain some different reasons why wars happen.
I can say which 20th century wars were most significant, and give reasons.

Ideologies: *ideas or beliefs that form the basis of a political or economic system*
Genocide: *the killing of an entire national, racial, religious, or ethnic group*

The twentieth century
Part 2: A changing world

The 20th century was a period of great change – change that took place much faster than at any time in human history. Let's look at some of those changes, and the impact they have had on the way we live.

1908 Henry Ford makes his first Model T car using an assembly line

1903 Wright brothers make the first manned flight

1924 Frozen food invented

1918 Women over 30 get the vote in Britain

1928 Antibiotics invented

1931 Empire State Building, New York, opens

1930s First holiday camps

1910

1930

1900

1920

1940

1912 Sinking of the Titanic

1918–19 Spanish Flu kills around 20 million people

1929–1939 The Great Depression leads to mass unemployment across the world

Getting you thinking

Think back over your own lifetime. What is the biggest change you can remember? How has that change affected your life? Now imagine if you were 100 years old. What changes would you have seen in your lifetime?

Study the timeline. It includes some of the inventions and events from the 20th century that the authors of this book think are important. Do you agree with their choice? Choose the *three* that you think have had the most impact and say why you have chosen them. Are the events you have chosen above the timeline or below it? Can you work out why some of the events are above the timeline, and some are below?

Now it's your turn

1. Can you group the events on the timeline into categories? Which categories would you use?
2. Does this lesson give a similar impression of the 20th century to the previous lesson? Can you explain any similarities and/or differences?
3. From the events on the timeline, would you say that the 20th century was one of 'progress'? Explain your answer.

Extension work

'Change = Progress'. Do you agree?

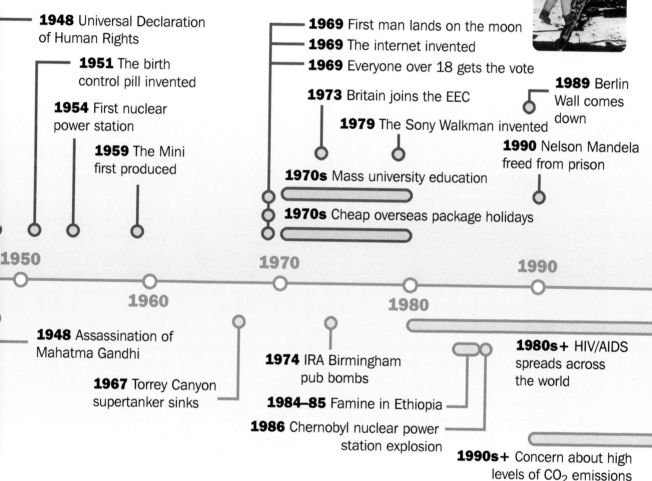

1948 Universal Declaration of Human Rights

1951 The birth control pill invented

1954 First nuclear power station

1959 The Mini first produced

1969 First man lands on the moon

1969 The internet invented

1969 Everyone over 18 gets the vote

1973 Britain joins the EEC

1979 The Sony Walkman invented

1989 Berlin Wall comes down

1990 Nelson Mandela freed from prison

1970s Mass university education

1970s Cheap overseas package holidays

1950

1960

1970

1980

1990

1948 Assassination of Mahatma Gandhi

1967 Torrey Canyon supertanker sinks

1974 IRA Birmingham pub bombs

1984–85 Famine in Ethiopia

1986 Chernobyl nuclear power station explosion

1980s+ HIV/AIDS spreads across the world

1990s+ Concern about high levels of CO_2 emissions

Check your progress

I can describe some of the major changes in the 20th century.
I can explain why changes might be for the better or for worse.
I can say which changes I think have had a major impact on the way we live, and why.

Christabel Thuburn, known as 'nana' to her family, was born on 10 December 1909, in Houghton-le-Spring, County Durham. She recently celebrated her 100th birthday.

Nana Christabel had two older brothers, who both served in the army. One of them, Stephen, was killed during World War Two when the Japanese blew up his ship in the Pacific ocean. In 1928, Nana married Matt, a coal miner. They lived with her parents until they could get a colliery house. The house had a range, which used coal for heating, cooking and hot water; a tin bath to use in front of the fire; and an outside toilet. Matt became the first person in the north-east to use a mechanised coal-cutter; he was sent around to other collieries to train miners how to use it. He lost a finger in an accident, and became a clerk above ground. He worked for 50 years in coal mining and died in 1973.

Nana Christabel and Grandad Matt, outside their first house

Nana had five children – four girls and a boy. Alice was the eldest. When she was two, Alice went to live with her grandma, and lived with her until her marriage in 1950. Nana was poorly with scarlet fever after having four children in quick succession and had to 'farm out' the children to relatives to look after – there was no social welfare in those days. Alice passed the 11-plus examination and went to grammar school. She paid for shorthand and typing classes in the evenings, and in 1944, when she was 16, she left school to work in an office in a Newcastle shipyard. She had to leave school without taking her 'O' Levels.

Nana now has grandchildren living in England, Scotland, France and Canada, and great-grandchildren dotted around the world, including Mauritius and Australia. When she was little, all her extended family lived within a few miles of each other, and most men worked in the coal industry. Nana thinks the greatest inventions of the 20th century are the telephone, which allows her to keep in touch with everybody, and the television. When she was younger though, she liked to dance to music on the wind-up gramophone her father bought.

Getting you thinking

Ian Dawson, an historian, has come up with these rules to help us understand the concept of significance. He argues that an event can be significant if it:

- changed events at the time
- improved many people's lives – or made them worse
- changed people's ideas
- had a long-lasting impact on their country or the world
- was a really good or a very bad example to other people of how to live or behave

What can be significant?	Example
Events	Genocide in Rwanda
People	Nelson Mandela
Developments	The atom bomb
Issues	The right to vote
Inventions	The television

Now it's your turn APP

1 Why should World War Two be remembered?
2 Using Ian Dawson's rules, which of the 20th century events you have looked at so far do you think was most significant?
3 Do you agree with Ian Dawson's rules? What rules for deciding on significance would you choose? Make a list.

Extension work

Using *your own rules for significance*, which event would you say had the most impact on the 20th century? Why?

Check your progress

I can say why I think an event might be significant to an historian.
I can apply Ian Dawson's rules to decide whether or not an event is significant.
I can create my own rules to decide whether or not an event is significant.

The Great War

Objectives

By the end of this unit you will know:

- why World War One happened
- what it was like to fight in the war
- what changes came about because of the war

Questions

1 Look at the photograph. In what ways does it:

   a) agree with the text?   **b)** disagree with the text?

2 Do you find anything surprising about the photograph?

3 The evidence on this page suggests that the French had nice, dry trenches, while the British had horrible, wet, muddy trenches. Do you think this is true?

4 What other information would you need to be able to answer this question properly?

5 Write down a list of questions you want to ask about World War One in the rest of this unit.

Before you study this unit, write down ten words that sum up what you already know about World War One.

World War One (1914–1918) shaped the 20th century. Some historians argue that the war was totally unexpected. Many men saw it as a great adventure, the chance to defend their country. Thinking the war would be over by Christmas, they rushed to join up – but it wasn't. The war soon became locked in a horrific stalemate, with neither side able to break through the other's defensive lines. Soon the trenches stretched from Switzerland in the south, to the Belgian coast in the north-west. The war became a deadly game of survival as soldiers struggled to dig trenches and avoid machine-gun fire and barbed wire. They lived, slept and died in mud, which was sometimes deep enough to drown in if they were not careful. Mud was almost as dangerous an enemy as the German army, especially in the British trenches.

French soldiers in a bomb-proof dugout

World War One: Mrs Beechey and her family

By 1918 the war had been going on for nearly four years. Millions of men had either volunteered or been called up (conscripted) to fight. Everyone had expected the war to be over by Christmas 1914. For the first time in a major war, nearly everyone in the country had been affected in some way.

Getting you thinking

The Beechey family in 1901

ROYAL VISIT TO LINCOLN

On 9 April 1918, King George V and Queen Mary visited Lincoln. The first visit of the day was to an aircraft factory. They went on to visit a tank factory, where the king insisted on being taken for a ride in a tank. The royal party then went on to the Guildhall where they were presented to local dignitaries. One of these was Mrs Amy Beechey.

Amy had 14 children, eight of whom were boys.

One of her daughters, Maud, had died of measles aged five, but all the others had lived into adulthood. All of the boys served in the war.

Mrs Beechey was presented to the king with the words: 'the widow of a Lincolnshire clergyman who had eight sons, five of whom have been killed during the war, one maimed, the other two now serving.' Their Majesties thanked Mrs Beechey for her sacrifice.

Dignitary: a person of high rank or position
Emigrate: leave your own country to go and live elsewhere

Barnard Beechey	born 1877	joined the Lincolnshire Regiment in August 1914. Killed in action, 1915.
Charles Beechey	born 1878	joined the Royal Fusiliers in 1916. Died of wounds, 1917.
Leonard Beechey	born 1881	a married man, conscripted in 1916. Died of wounds, 1917.
Christopher Beechey	born 1883	*emigrated* to Western Australia, joined the Australian Imperial Infantry at the outbreak of war. Invalided out of the army, 1915.
Frank Beechey	born 1886	joined the Lincolnshire Regiment in September 1914. Died of wounds, 1916.
Eric Beechey	born 1889	trained to be a dentist, joined the Royal Army Medical Corps.
Harold Beechey	born 1891	also emigrated to Western Australia with Christopher, joined up in September 1914. Killed in action, 1917.
Samuel Beechey	born 1899	called up in 1918 and served on the Western Front for the final three weeks of the war.

The war did not just affect individual families; whole communities were affected too. In its early months, groups of friends and neighbours often volunteered for the army together. The Accrington Pals *Battalion* (11th Battalion East Lancashire Regiment) all came from Accrington and the surrounding area – a whole battalion joined up in September 1914. They spent nearly two years training, before arriving in France to take part in the Battle of the Somme, July 1916. In the first hour of the attack the Accrington Pals went '*over the top*,' to be met by German machine-gun fire. Out of the 720 Accrington Pals who took part in the attack, 584 were killed, wounded or reported missing.

Now it's your turn

1 How might Mrs Beechey have felt as more and more of her sons joined the army?
2 What do you think she felt as more of her sons were killed?
3 What might Mrs Beechey have replied to the king when he thanked her for her sacrifice?
4 What do you think the people of Accrington felt when they heard the news about the casualties at the Somme?

Check your progress

I can talk about how a mother might feel when her son enlisted in the army at the start of a war.

I can try to imagine how a mother might feel when her son is killed in action.

I can imagine the impact on a town or village when it suffers many casualties at once.

Battalion: fighting unit of around 1,000 men
Over the top: leaving the British trenches to attack the German trenches

What stories lie behind our war memorials?

Objectives

By the end of this lesson you will be able to:

- tell some personal stories about the war from the evidence available
- use the evidence to reach conclusions about the nature of war

Nearly every town and village in the UK has at least one war memorial *commemorating* those who were killed fighting for their country during World War One. The memorials are often a good way to start to explore the war. Let's think about both what they tell us about the men and women whose names they list, and what can they tell us about the war itself.

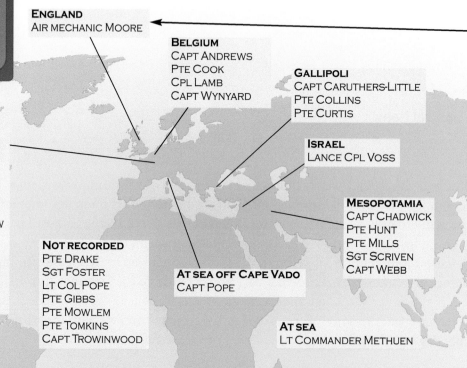

ENGLAND
AIR MECHANIC MOORE

BELGIUM
CAPT ANDREWS
PTE COOK
CPL LAMB
CAPT WYNYARD

GALLIPOLI
CAPT CARUTHERS-LITTLE
PTE COLLINS
PTE CURTIS

FRANCE
PTE MAYO
2ND LT CHADWICK
LANCE CPL CURTIS
PTE EASLEY
LT COL HAIG BROWN
PTE HARE
LT HILL
MAJ HUGHES ONSLOW
PTE MEMBURY
PTE PINK
2ND LT POPE
PTE SARGENT
CPL TREW
2ND LT WILLIS

ISRAEL
LANCE CPL VOSS

MESOPOTAMIA
CAPT CHADWICK
PTE HUNT
PTE MILLS
SGT SCRIVEN
CAPT WEBB

NOT RECORDED
PTE DRAKE
SGT FOSTER
LT COL POPE
PTE GIBBS
PTE MOWLEM
PTE TOMKINS
CAPT TROWINWOOD

AT SEA OFF CAPE VADO
CAPT POPE

AT SEA
LT COMMANDER METHUEN

TO THE GLORY OF GOD AND IN PROUD MEMORY OF THESE MEMBERS OF OUR CHURCH & PARISH WHO DIED FOR US IN THE GREAT WAR

REMEMBER THEM IN YOUR PRAYERS AND IN YOUR LIVES

War memorial on the side of St Mary's Roman Catholic church, Dorchester

Commemorating: remembering

Getting you thinking

Look carefully at the war memorial in the photograph at the bottom of the opposite page. It is on the side of St Mary's Roman Catholic church in Dorchester; it commemorates those killed during World War One who were also members of the church. This suggests that there are other war memorials and other deaths commemorated elsewhere in Dorchester.

How many different regiments can you identify on the memorial? How many different services (army, navy etc) can you find? Why might someone from the Indian Army have died in Dorchester?

Extension work

Find your local war memorial or memorials – there may be more than one in your town or village. Make a list of the names that appear on it and then choose one or two of the servicemen. As with the example of Harold Moore, see if you can find out where they served and when and how they died. Say whether or not you find memorials useful for finding out about the war.

Air Mechanic Harold Moore was 19 when he died. Using the Commonwealth War Graves Commission website (www.cwgc.org), we discovered that he was in the Royal Naval Air Service (RNAS), working with airship C11. He died on 21 July 1917 and is buried in Dorchester Cemetery. He was born and brought up in Dorchester, but how did he become part of the RNAS? And what was airship C11 doing in July 1917? In fact, what part did airships play in the war? Sometimes the evidence raises as many questions as it provides answers.

The book 'Battlebags: British Airships of the Great War' by Ces Mowthorpe, gives us the following information about airship C11:

…built at Kingsnorth, Isle of Grain, Kent. Air Trials were carried out on 9th June 1916. To Howden, (main RNAS airship base, Yorkshire) 26th June 1916, damaged propeller when landing. Wrecked at Scarborough, 23rd April 1917, with no fatalities. The airship was rebuilt at Howden and re-named C11. It burst into flames over the River Humber on 21st July 1917. All five men on board were killed.

Ces Mowthorpe, 'Battlebags: British Airships of the Great War'

Now it's your turn

1 Using the details on the photograph, plot a graph of casualties in the war, year by year. When did most servicemen die? When did fewest die?
2 Using the map and the dates on the war memorial can you suggest a chronology for the war – i.e. where was most fighting happening in which years?
3 How useful do you now think a local war memorial is when studying World War One?

Check your progress

I can find a story from a war memorial.
I can use a war memorial as the starting point for further research into World War One.
I can draw some conclusions about World War One from a war memorial.

Short-term causes of the war: assassination in Sarajevo

Objectives

By the end of this lesson you will be able to:

- explore the causes of the *assassination* of Archduke Franz Ferdinand
- think about whether breaking the law is ever justified

Archduke Franz Ferdinand was the heir to the throne of Austria-Hungary. On the 28 June 1914, he and his wife were on a state visit to the town of Sarajevo in Bosnia. He was there to review the troops on their summer exercises and to meet the people.

Getting you thinking

In 1908 Bosnia had been taken over by Austria-Hungary. Some people in Bosnia did not want to be part of Austria-Hungary; they thought that Bosnia should be part of neighbouring Serbia, and they were prepared to kill to achieve their aims. Among them was a student called Gavrillo Princip; he was dying of tuberculosis, so he felt he had nothing to lose. He had only ever fired a gun once before, and then he had missed the target.

Archduke Franz Ferdinand arriving in Sarajevo

Assassination: the killing of a public figure
Black Hand Gang: terrorists who wanted Bosnia to be part of Serbia

It was a hot summer's day. According to newspaper reports, huge crowds lined the streets as the archduke was driven into town. Among the crowds were several members of the *Black Hand Gang*, armed with bombs and pistols; it was their intention to kill Franz Ferdinand. On the way to City Hall, one of the assassins politely asked a policeman which car was carrying the archduke. He then threw a bomb at the archduke's car, which bounced off it and exploded, injuring several military officers in the car behind. At City Hall the archduke was persuaded to leave the city as soon as possible, but no-one told the driver. On the way out of the city, the driver followed the original route, where he was stopped by an official and told to use the new route. Unfortunately, the car stopped right beside one of the assassins, Gavrillo Princip, who stepped forward and fired twice, at point blank range, killing both Franz Ferdinand and his wife

The Balkans in 1914

The *Balkans* had been part of the Ottoman Empire for 500 years. The previous fifty years had seen a series of wars between the Balkan states as the Ottoman Empire weakened and they each tried to win back their independence. Austria took over Bosnia in 1908 to try to prevent minorities in Austria-Hungary from gaining their independence too. Franz Ferdinand wanted the *minorities* in Austria-Hungary to run some of their own affairs, but not have independence. June 28 was a very special day for Serbians, as it was the anniversary of a famous battle, the Battle of Kosovo in 1389, when Serbia lost its independence to the Ottomans.

Now it's your turn

1 The newspapers reported that huge crowds greeted Franz Ferdinand, which suggests that he was very popular. In what ways does the photograph support the newspaper accounts?
2 Do you think it was wise for Franz Ferdinand to visit Sarajevo, and to go there on 28 June?
3 Why do you think Franz Ferdinand was killed?

Extension work

1 Was Gavrillo Princip justified in assassinating Franz Ferdinand?
2 Is it ever right to kill someone?
3 Is it ever right to break the law?

Check your progress

☆ I can pick out contradictions between two different types of evidence.
☆☆ I can give some reasons for the assassination of Franz Ferdinand.
☆☆☆ I can discuss when it might be acceptable to break the law.

The Balkans: part of southeast Europe
Minorities: small groups within a population

The calm before the storm

It was a glorious summer. Throughout June and July 1914, Europe basked in a prolonged heat wave. Seaside towns were crowded with visitors. *Butlers* and servants across the continent prepared for their employers' usual hunting expeditions, holidays, spas and cures in the summer months.

Getting you thinking

In the summer of 1914, Europe seemed to be at peace. In fact, relations between the *Great Powers* seemed better than they had been for many years. Britain and Germany were putting aside their differences after years of tense naval rivalry. The French were no longer so hostile to the Germans over their loss of Alsace-Lorraine in the *Franco-Prussian War* of 1870–71. Although the weakness of the Turkish (Ottoman) Empire had created real instability in the Balkans, Austria-Hungary and Russia had not allowed the conflicts there in 1912 and 1913 to draw them into war.

Europe in 1914

Great Powers: Germany, Austria-Hungary, Russia, France and Britain
Butler: personal servant

The only cloud on the horizon was the assassination of the heir to the throne of the Austro-Hungarian Empire, Archduke Franz Ferdinand, in Sarajevo on 28 June. Even this did not seem to shatter the peace. A world war was simply unimaginable in the summer of 1914. After all, nearly all the European heads of state were related by blood or marriage. They met often and exchanged correspondence that began, for example, 'Dear Cousin Nicky'. In any case, assassinations were not unusual in the Balkans, and Franz Ferdinand was not a popular man in Austria–Hungary.

So, instead of going to war, Europe's leaders went on holiday. The German emperor, the Kaiser, went on his usual yachting holiday in the Norwegian fiords. His chief minister went on his usual shooting party; the acting head of the German foreign office went on honeymoon. The French leaders went on a ceremonial visit to Russia by sea, out of contact with their government, only arriving back in Paris on 29 July. Meanwhile, Britain's foreign secretary, Sir Edward Gray, went trout fishing, and the first sea lord, Winston Churchill, retreated to a Norfolk beach to build sandcastles with his children.

The Russian Tsar and his family spent a carefree July at their summer palace on the Gulf of Finland. 'Every day', Nicholas II noted in his diary, 'we play tennis or swim in the fiords.' Even the aged emperor of Austria-Hungary, Franz Josef, passed July at his summer residence, to take the waters and the mountain air. As the historian John Keegan has said, 'In 1914 … war came out of a cloudless sky.'

The garden party of a wealthy family in the summer of 1914

So, why did a single act of terrorism, in a part of Europe which most people had not even heard of, lead to a world war six weeks later?

Now it's your turn

1 What were the factors working against war in the summer of 1914? Draw a spidergram showing the positive links between the Great Powers.
2 From what you have read, would you have expected war to break out in August 1914?
3 Draw up a table, like the one below, sorting the evidence into two columns:

Evidence in favour of peace	Evidence in favour of war

Check your progress

I can say why I think war was unlikely in the summer of 1914.

I can sort the evidence I have into two groups – in favour of peace and in favour of war.

I can use the evidence to make a convincing argument about the likelihood of war in summer 1914.

Franco-Prussian War: a war between France and Prussia in 1870-1871, won by Prussia

What were the long-term causes of the war?

Objectives

By the end of this lesson you will be able to:

- explore the causes of World War One
- think about the relative importance of long-term and short-term causes

In the years that followed [1901] the peoples of Western Europe and America were becoming consumers rather than soldiers. They looked forward to more progress, more prosperity, more peace ... For those who were well-off, the world was freer than it is today. You could go practically anywhere ... You needed no passports, and many had none.

David Fromkin, 'Europe's Last Summer: Who started the Great War in 1914?'

Getting you thinking

Britain • Germany • Austria-Hungary • Russia • Japan • Ottoman Empire • Italy • France

1902 · 1907 · 1882 · 1873 · 1882 · 1691–83 · 1882 · 1907 · 1900–02

Alliances between the Great Powers before World War One

Look at all the countries in the cartoon. They represent the Great Powers, the leading countries in the world, in 1914. What point is the cartoonist trying to make? What does this tell us about relations between the Great Powers in 1914?

According to the cartoonist, the world is split into two groups, or *alliances*. Who is on which side? Do alliances make war more likely or less likely?

Why do you think the Ottoman Empire is shown outside the two groups?

Consumer: someone who buys goods to use for themselves

British and German navies compared, 1914

Type of ship	UK	Germany
Dreadnoughts	24	13
Battle-cruisers	10	6
Pre-Dreadnought battleships	38	30
Cruisers	47	14
Light cruisers	61	35
Destroyers	225	152
Submarines	76	30

The Arms race
Money spent on arms by the major powers 1883–1913 (millions of £)

Britain	1883	25
	1908	59
	1913	77
France	1883	31
	1908	44
	1913	82
Russia	1883	36
	1908	60
	1913	92
Germany	1883	20
	1908	59
	1913	100
Austria-Hungary	1883	13
	1908	21
	1913	24
Italy	1883	12
	1908	18
	1913	29

Following the assassination of Franz Ferdinand on 28 June, Austria-Hungary, with the support of Germany, issued an ultimatum to Serbia. Serbia had to accept Austrian control in running Serbia or Austria would declare war. Russia offered to help Serbia and began to *mobilise*. Austria declared war on Serbia on 28 July. On 1 August, Germany declared war on Russia, and then on 3 August, declared war on France. Faced with war against both France and Russia, Germany immediately carried out the Schlieffen Plan. This was intended to prevent Germany having to fight a war on two fronts: it would first attack and quickly defeat France, then be free to fight Russia. Germany invaded Belgium in 1914 as the first stage in this plan. Britain, bound – like Germany – by the Convention of 1839 to protect Belgium, declared war on Germany on 4 August. Within little more than a week, like a line of dominoes, most of the world was at war.

Italy had an alliance with Germany and Austria-Hungary, and was expected to enter any war on their side. Once war broke out Italy remained neutral, staying out of the war until 1915. Italy then joined the war on the side of Britain and France, who had promised it land from Austria-Hungary when the war was over.

Japan had an alliance with Britain and hoped to capture Germany's colonies in the Pacific area once the war was over.

Now it's your turn

1 Do the figures for 'money spent on arms' and the message of the cartoon agree with David Fromkin's arguments about the likelihood of war?

2 Using the sources, how long do you think the Great Powers had been preparing for war?

3 Who, in your opinion, was to blame for World War One?

Check your progress

I can sort the causes of World War One into long-term causes and short-term causes.
I can decide which causes I think are the most important.
I can use the evidence I have to make a convincing case about the causes of World War One.

Alliance: *coalition of countries agreeing to work together for the same aims*
Mobilise: *make armies ready for war*

Joining up!

Objectives

By the end of this lesson you will be able to:

- explore the motives of people who joined the army in 1914
- find out if people in different countries felt the same way about the war that year

In August 1914, thousands and thousands of young men in every country rushed to join the army. They thought that the war would be 'over by Christmas' and wanted to make sure they joined up before it was too late.

Getting you thinking

In the boxes are stories of men who fought in the Great War. Why do you think so many people chose to volunteer?

Private George Morgan

We had been brought up to believe that Britain was the best country in the world and we wanted to defend her. The history taught us at school showed that we were better than other people and now all the news was that Germany was the aggressors and we wanted to show the Germans what we could do. I thought it would be the end of the world if I didn't pass the medical. I was only sixteen and rather small. It was marvellous being accepted. When I went back home and told my mother she said I was a fool and she'd give me a good hiding…

A group of volunteer shipyard workers on parade in Belfast, 1914

Aggressors: *the people responsible for starting a war*
Compulsion: *being forced to do something*

Alan Seeger

Alan Seeger was an American who went to live in Paris in 1912. On 24 August 1914 he joined the French Foreign Legion to fight for the Allies in World War One. He served on the Western Front. As he was about to move to the front, he wrote: 'I go into action with the lightest of light hearts. The hard work has not broken but hardened me, and I am in excellent health and spirits ... I am happy and full of excitement over the wonderful days that are ahead.'

Talking about other American volunteers in his unit he said: 'Their case is little known, even by the French. They are foreigners on whom the outbreak of war laid no formal compulsion. But they had stood, and looked out over the lights of Paris. Paris was in peril. Were they not under a moral obligation ... to put their breasts between her and destruction?'

Alan Seeger was killed at the Battle of the Somme, in July 1916.

Heinrich Plesker

Heinrich Plesker was born on 21 September 1882 in Coesfeld, Germany, the son of a small farmer with a large family. Before the war he worked as a labourer and did his compulsory two-year military service. He then drove a horse and cart for the Coesfeld soap-factory. Finally he joined the Royal Prussian State Railways as a labourer. On 24 May 1913 he married Gertrud Kock, and nine months later they had a baby girl. Not long after the Great War began, Heinrich was called up as a reservist. Heinrich was not a young recruit, but an 'old man' when he went to war. He served as stretcher-bearer in the 1st company of the Reserve Infantry Regiment No 216.

Heinrich Plesker was killed just one day before his third wedding anniversary, in May 1916.

Now it's your turn

1 Look carefully at the photograph. What does it tell you about the kind of people who volunteered for the British Army in 1914?
2 Why did George, Alan and Heinrich join the army?
3 How are their reasons similar?
4 How are their reasons different?

Check your progress

I can say why young men joined the British Army in 1914.

I can see similarities and differences in the reasons young men joined up in different countries.

I can say why the war was so popular in 1914.

Reservist: someone who has served in the army and who will be called up again if war breaks out

Cowardice or bravery?

Objectives

By the end of this lesson you will:

- find out why some men refused to fight in World War One
- learn how these men were treated

At the start of World War One, many thousands of men volunteered to fight. But by late 1915, it was clear that even the large number of volunteers joining the army would not be enough. More men were needed. So in early 1916 the government passed the Military Service Act, introducing conscription. All men between the ages of 18 and 41 could now be forced to join up and fight.

Getting you thinking

Some men refused to join up. They were called conscientious objectors because their consciences would not allow them to fight. Some refused for religious reasons, as the Bible said 'Thou shalt not kill'. Others held strong political views and thought it wrong to shoot at their working-class 'brothers'. Nicknamed 'conchies', about 16,000 were registered as conscientious objectors by the end of the war.

The most effective recruiting agents ... were the women and girls who handed out white feathers to men not in uniform and not wearing a war service badge.

Source W. H. A. Groom, 'Poor Bloody Infantry: a memoir of the First World War' (1976)

A group of conscientious objectors protest against the war

CONSCIENTIOUS OBJECTORS TO MILITARY SERVICE

Commuted: changed, substituted

Anyone who refused the call-up had to face a special court called a military tribunal. Some, who managed to convince the court of their beliefs, were willing to perform other kinds of army service. They were given ambulance work or drivers' duties. Many were sent to the front as stretcher bearers, where they faced the same risks as all the other troops, and sometimes worse, as they carried wounded men back from No-Man's Land.

Some conscientious objectors, however, refused to do any form of military work. Known as 'absolutists', and generally regarded as cowards and shirkers, they were shown no sympathy by the military tribunals. The vast majority were conscripted. They were then court-martialled when they refused to obey an officer's orders. Almost all were sent to prisons or labour camps. One group of 35 was sent to France, court-martialled and sentenced to death, although this was afterwards *commuted* to ten years' hard labour.

Life in the prisons and the camps was dreadful. Inmates were beaten, kept in *solitary confinement* in filthy cells on a diet of bread and water, and they were frequently not allowed to talk. Punishments were severe. Some men were suspended by the wrists from a rope, so that their feet dangled above the ground. Others were put into wooden cages like animals. Some were thrown naked into sewage ponds or kept in pits in the ground. Of the 6,261 who were sentenced in this way, over 70 died from their treatment and more than 30 went mad.

And after the war life for conscientious objectors was still miserable. They stood no chance of getting a job and they were despised and jeered at by former workmates and friends, neighbours and even their own families.

Extension work

Do you think men and women have a right not to fight for their country? Explain your answer.

Now it's your turn   APP

1   Why did some men refuse to join the army?
2   How were these men treated?
3   Why do you think the government went to so much trouble to deal with conscientious objectors in this way?
4   Do you think people who are prepared to stand up for their beliefs should be admired? Explain your answer.

Check your progress

I can talk about why some men might choose not to fight for their country.
I can describe the different things that conscientious objectors did during the war.
I can describe how conscientious objectors were treated by other people during the war, and afterwards.

Solitary confinement: a kind of imprisonment in which the prisoner is completely alone, with no contact with other people

What was it like in the trenches?

Objectives

By the end of this lesson you will be able to:

- say what it was like in the trenches
- use the evidence you have to challenge an interpretation of life in the trenches

An Indian soldier in the British Army keeps watch on the German trenches

Following the failure of the Schlieffen Plan [see page 23] both the Allies and the Germans 'dug in' to try to stabilise the front line. Trenches stretched all the way from the Swiss border to the North Sea. The position of these trenches hardly changed over the next four years.

Getting you thinking

Only about one in ten soldiers would be in the front line at any one time. Soldiers usually spent four days in the front line, four days in the support trenches and four days in reserve.

The first thing soldiers had to do in a trench was to make themselves safe from attack. Then they had to live. Everything they needed had to be brought up from the rear, usually at night.
It was much too dangerous to move around in daylight near the front line.

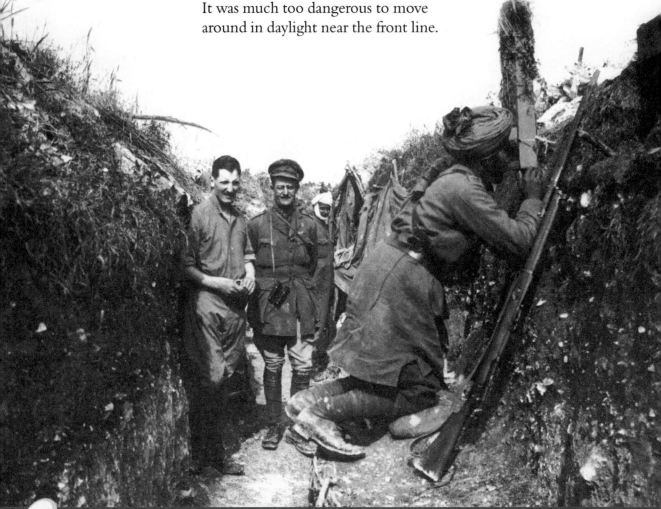

Pilfered: stole

During the last three days the weather has continued very wet. Continual work is required to keep the trenches dry and to prevent the earth from falling in.

Source 1 *Daily Record and Mail, 6 January 1915*

The outstanding feature of this part of the front was the extraordinary number of rats. They grew fat on the food they pilfered from us. One night a rat ran across my face. Unfortunately, my mouth happened to be open and the hind legs of the filthy little beast went right in…

Source 2 *A. Stuart Dolden, 'Cannon Fodder' (1980)*

One blanket per man was the issue for sleeping, and Phillips and I found it beneficial to sleep together, and share our blankets and greatcoats … Wanting to wash next morning we found that the only water was in the ditches and shell-holes near the camp…

Source 4 *Frank Dunham, 'The Long Carry: the War Diary of a Stretcher-Bearer' (1973)*

Ration parties from each company went to carry back the rations which were tied in sandbags and consisted, usually, of bread, hard biscuits, tinned meat, tinned jam, tinned butter, sugar and tea, pork and beans, cigarettes and tobacco. Water was sent up the line in petrol cans. The medical officer was responsible for ensuring all drinking water was chlorinated. In winter there was a ration of rum…

Source 3 *Malcolm Brown, 'Tommy Goes to War' (1990)*

…For the majority of soldiers actual living conditions in and behind the lines on quiet sectors were little if any worse than in peacetime. Certainly many British soldiers enjoyed a better diet, better medical care and better welfare than they had as civilians.

Source 5 *Correlli Barnett, 'The Great War' (2009)*

Now it's your turn

1 What, in your opinion, was the greatest difficulty in the trenches?
2 Do the other sources support Correlli Barnett's interpretation that many soldiers enjoyed a better diet than in civilian life?

Extension work

Do you think soldiers enjoyed being in the trenches? Explain your answer.

Check your progress

I can describe some aspects of life in the trenches.
I can use evidence to support my conclusion.
I can decide which pieces of evidence support and which challenge an interpretation.

Why did so many soldiers die in the war?

Objectives

By the end of this lesson you will be able to:

- see how technology changed warfare
- think about the impact of technology on warfare

The standard British infantry weapon at the start of World War One was the Lee Enfield Mark III rifle, introduced in 1907. With it, a trained soldier could accurately fire up to 25 rounds every minute. It remained in use throughout the war, with minor modifications.

Once both sides were established in trenches, they strengthened their defences and developed new weapons to try to help their soldiers capture enemy trenches.

Getting you thinking

MACHINE GUNS

- At the start of the war, each British army battalion had two machine guns. In 1915 this was increased to four.
- A machine-gun crew of two men could fire up to 600 rounds of ammunition per minute.
- It took six other men to keep the gun supplied with water and ammunition.
- They were a superb defensive weapon, especially when sited in a strongpoint or pillbox.
- Later they were mounted successfully on tanks and aircraft.

GAS

- The Germans were the first to use a large-scale gas attack in January 1915, on the Eastern Front against the Russian army.
- There were several types of gas – tear gas and mustard gas were designed to incapacitate troops, while chlorine and phosgene were designed to kill.
- Gas masks were developed to protect troops from the effects of gas.
- Early gas attacks depended on the wind to deliver the gas into the enemy's trenches.
- Over one million men became casualties as a result of poison gas, although most survived.

AIRCRAFT

- The introduction of aircraft transformed war.
- At first they were used as spotters for the artillery, picking out enemy targets.
- Once the machine gun was developed to fire forward through the propeller, fighter aircraft appeared, shooting down enemy planes.
- Later in the war, big four-engined planes were developed to bomb enemy cities.
- By 1918 the Royal Air Force had over 22,500 planes in operation.

Strongpoint: specially strengthened defensive position
Pillbox: concrete shelter for machine guns

A tank on the Amiens Road on the Western Front, August 1918

TANK

- First introduced, by Britain, in 1916, tanks were slow and unreliable.
- Bulletproof and able to cross rough ground and trenches, they could crush barbed wire and destroy machine gun strongpoints.
- With a crew of eight men, they were either 'female' with five machine guns, or 'male' with two six-pounder guns.
- Average speed was only 4 mph.

- Tanks were very uncomfortable to fight in. Temperatures inside them could reach 38°C. They were noisy and likely to get blown up by a direct hit.
- At Amiens, in August 1918, over 600 tanks were used by the British in what was the biggest tank campaign of the war.

Now it's your turn

1 Do you think these new weapons made it easier to defend a trench, or attack it?
2 Which of these new weapons do you think had the most impact on trench warfare?
3 Do you think technology on its own could have won the war?

Extension work

Design a weapon that you think might have made it easier to capture German trenches during World War One.

Check your progress

I can talk about new inventions introduced during World War One.
I can understand the part played by technology during the war.
I can say whether I think the new inventions helped attackers or defenders.

Incapacitate: injure but not kill

An air raid on Britain

Objectives

By the end of this lesson you will be able to:

- examine differing points of view about the same event
- question the effectiveness of World War One bombing raids

Zeppelins were airships with a rigid metal skeleton, enclosed by a huge skin or envelope; on the inside there were separate 'gas bags' containing hydrogen, a gas which is lighter than air. The Germans used the airships to bomb Britain during World War One, but out of a total of 115 zeppelins used, 77 were either destroyed or so badly damaged that they could not be used again. In June 1917 the German military stopped using zeppelins for bombing raids over Britain.

Lieutenant William Leefe Robinson last night became the first member of the Royal Flying Corps to shoot down one of the German airships that have been bombing England since the war broke out. The raider was caught in search-lights above Hatfield, Hertfordshire. Despite not being able to climb as high as the raider, Lt. Robinson emptied his Lewis gun into the tail of the raider which burst into flames and crashed. Lt. Robinson has been awarded the VC for his brave and courageous action. Last night was the first time British planes have been able to shoot down one of these raiders.

Source 1 *From a newspaper account, 3 September 1916*

London Underground poster during the time of the German zeppelin raids, by the artist Frank Brangwyn

It was a fantastic sight, like a big silver cigar, and it seemed to be going very slowly by this time. A lot of people came out of their houses and then all of a sudden flames started to come from the zeppelin and then it broke in half and was one mass of flames. It was an incredible sight: people were cheering, dancing, singing and somebody started playing the bagpipes. This went on well into the night.

Source 2 *Ten-year old Henry Tuttle remembers the first downing of a zeppelin.*

Extension work

How effective were zeppelins as bombers during World War One?

To me it was what I would call an awful sight. It was like a big cigar I suppose and all of the bag part had caught fire – the gas part. I mean – it was roaring flames; blue, red, purple ... And we knew that there were about sixty people in it – we'd always been told there was a crew of about sixty – and that they were being roasted to death. Of course you weren't supposed to feel any pity for your enemies, nevertheless I was appalled to see the kind, good-hearted British people dancing about in the streets at the sight of sixty people being burned alive – clapping and singing and cheering. When I said I was appalled that anyone could be pleased to see such a terrible sight they said; 'But they're Germans; they're the enemy – not human beings.

Source 3 *Sybil Morrison remembers the first downing of a zeppelin*

Now it's your turn

1. What do these two eyewitness accounts add to the story of Lieutenant Robinson's Victoria Cross?
2. What do they tell us about ordinary people's views of zeppelins and/or Germans?
3. Do we now have a complete story of the event?

Check your progress

I can talk about what zeppelins were and how they were used.
I can understand the impact that zeppelin raids had on some English people.
I can understand that the same event can be seen in different ways by different people on the same side of a war.

Appalled: really upset

How did life on the home front affect women?

Objectives

By the end of this lesson you will be able to:

- explore the impact of the war on life in Britain
- decide how important the role played by women in the war effort was

During World War One, over six million men were *mobilised*, mostly to fight overseas. The war caused many changes in society and the way the country was run. Government regulations controlled the news, what people could say, hours and wages – even the hours pubs could stay open. Britain came close to becoming a dictatorship.

Getting you thinking

During the war prices rose by around 100 per cent, but so too did wages. Many people had more money than ever before. Wages could be as high as £5 per week for women munitions workers making shells for the war effort. This was much higher than pre-war wages for servants and shop girls. But the wealth came at a price: long shifts of 12 hours a day, six days a week. Yet despite dangerous conditions handling explosives, *noxious* fumes and hard physical labour, there was no shortage of volunteers.

Women employed as post office workers during the First World War

Mobilised: called up to fight in the armed forces

The worst factory accident was at Silvertown, in the East End of London. On 19 January 1917, the munitions factory exploded. The fires could be seen 30 miles away in Essex. 69 people were killed and over 400 injured. There was extensive damage to the area around the factory. It was estimated that 60–70,000 properties in the vicinity were damaged in some way.

It wasn't just in factories that women were *indispensable*. Over 270,000 worked in the Women's Land Army, growing food that could no longer be imported. Over 650,000 worked in government offices, and more than 100,000 as nurses. In any job where men had gone off to war, you would find women taking their places. By 1918 nearly five million women were working in industry and commerce, most of them in jobs that would have been closed to women before the war.

Food was often in short supply as German submarines – known as U-boats – sank ships transporting food to Britain. As a result, rationing was introduced in January 1918, to make sure that everyone had enough to eat.

Not only did women have to work long hours and find enough to eat, they became, in effect, single-parent families who had to look after their children too.

> World War One had an enormous impact on living standards, both in terms of poverty and health, improving the lot of many of the nation's poorest citizens. Next, through their war work, women gained a profile and rights in society that had previously been denied to them ... Finally, in general, the home front idea was a great social leveller and acted as a stimulus to wider social reform after the war.
>
> Peter Craddick-Adams, BBC History website

Now it's your turn

1 Do you think the war made women's lives easier, or harder?
2 How important do you think the role of women was during World War One?
3 Do you agree with Peter Craddick-Adams about the three main gains women made in the war?
4 Some historians argue that it was because of their contribution to war work that women over 30 were given the vote in 1918. What do you think?

Check your progress

I can suggest ways in which World War One impacted on the way Britain was governed.
I can understand how the war affected women's lives.
I can judge an historian's interpretation of the impact of war on women.

Indispensable: absolutely necessary
Home front: the work of people at home in Britain in support of the war effort

Sapper Martin goes home on leave

Objectives

By the end of this lesson you will be able to:

- discover how soldiers felt about leave
- discuss how reliable diaries are as evidence

Jack Martin was 31 when he was *called up* in January 1916. He joined the Royal Engineers and became a signaller. Soldiers were not supposed to keep diaries, but throughout his service, until February 1919, Martin kept a secret diary, telling no-one. It was discovered by his son in 1999 and has recently been published.

Why do you think soldiers were forbidden to keep diaries? Why do you think Jack kept his diary secret until he died?

Getting you thinking

6 October 1917
Up very early and packed everything in readiness. Got away soon after 9am. Tramped to the crossroads and then jumped a lorry which took me nearly to the Rest Camp where I reported. We left at 2.30 and caught a train from Bray station to Boulogne. It was a long and slow journey. Packed 30-40 to a truck; it was impossible to lie down. We finally got on board about 11am, and the boat left around 12.15. Arrived in Folkestone about 3.15, and got to Victoria at 6pm. On to 17 Hastings Road, where Elsie was alone. She had a feeling that I would come. Slept at no 76 on a real bed with real sheets and a soft pillow.

8 October 1917
At Ealing seeing old friends.

10 October 1917
To Kings Lynn with Elsie to see Lil, Edward and Peggy.

13 October 1917
From Kings Lynn to Dunmow with Elsie. Was glad to see my mother again. 15 October 1917 Returned to Ealing with Elsie. The time is passing quickly.

18 October 1917
Up early and Elsie came with me. It was very hard to say 'goodbye,' but she is a brave little girl and gave me a bright smile as we parted. Train to Folkestone. After several hours of dreary waiting we boarded the boat for Boulogne...

7 June 1918
Leave has been increased slightly, bringing my chances from Xmas 1920 to the autumn of 1919. It is always an engaging occupation to calculate when your leave will come round...

11 October 1918
The truly joyful news has arrived! I am to cross over [the channel] next Tuesday (15th). Hooray! I am as wibbly-wobbly as a blancmange

Diary extracts from 'Sapper Martin: The Secret Great War Diary of Jack Martin'

Called up: conscripted

Now it's your turn

1 Why might Sapper Martin feel 'all wibbly-wobbly as a blancmange' about the prospect of going on leave?
2 Does the diary give the impression that everything was done to make leave as pleasant as possible for soldiers?
3 Sapper Martin kept his diary a secret, even after his death. Does this make the contents more useful to us as evidence of the way soldiers felt on the Western Front, or less useful? Explain your answer.

Extension work

Sapper Martin was engaged to Elsie, but they had agreed not to get married until the war was over and he came home for good. Why might they have agreed this? Do you think it was a good idea or not? Do you think having Elsie 'waiting at home' made it easier for Sapper Martin while he was at the front, or harder?

British troops coming home for Christmas leave, December 1916

Check your progress

⭐ I can suggest why leave was so important for soldiers.
⭐⭐ I can obtain evidence from a diary in support of my *hypothesis*.
⭐⭐⭐ I can describe how diaries can be used as historical sources, and some possible limitations.

Hypothesis: an idea of what might be true for which you need to find evidence

Attack on the Somme, 1916

Objectives

By the end of this lesson you will be able to:

- explore reasons for the failure of the Battle of the Somme
- explore reasons for Haig being known as 'Butcher of the Somme'

General Douglas Haig became commander-in-chief of the British forces on the Western Front from December 1915.

Getting you thinking

In an attempt to break the *stalemate* on the Western Front and relieve the pressure on the French at *Verdun*, Haig ordered the Somme offensive on 1 July 1916. The attack was led by the New Army – all those volunteers from August 1914 who had been training for 18 months. Heavy shelling should have smashed the German barbed wire and destroyed machine gun posts. After a week's bombardment, waves of men went over the top, only to be mown down by machine guns and caught up in the barbed wire. Haig had believed that a frontal assault would punch a hole through the German lines and allow the British to break through and win.

British troops of the Middlesex Regiment wheeling their wounded comrades along a muddy road from the Somme trenches, November 1916

Stalemate: *neither side winning or losing*
Verdun: *major battle on the Western Front between Germany and France in June 1916*

The British Army suffered 60,000 *casualties* (just under 20,000 of whom were killed) on the first day, the highest in its history. The 801 men from the 1st Newfoundland Regiment attacked that day; only 68 made it out unharmed while over 500 died. Haig continued to order more attacks until the offensive was called off in November 1916, when the British had advanced six miles, and both sides had suffered a total of over 1.5 million casualties. Haig's conduct of the battle made him one of the most controversial figures of the war.

...the total casualties are estimated at over 40,000 to date. This cannot be considered severe in view of the numbers engaged, and the length of front attacked.

Haig's diary, 2 July 1916

I did not believe then, and I do not believe now, that the enormous casualties were justified. Throughout the war huge bombardments failed again and again yet we persisted in employing the same hopeless method of attack...

Charles Hudson from 'Soldier, Poet, Rebel' (2007)

...It is the story of the million who would rather die than be thought of as cowards and also of the two or three individuals who would rather the million perish than that they as leaders should admit that they were blunderers...

David Lloyd George, Britain's prime minister, writing in his war memoirs, published after the war

The military commanders had no respect for human life. General Haig cared nothing about casualties. Of course, he was carrying out government policy...

Lieutenant James Lovegrove, Royal North Lancashire Regiment. Lovegrove, a lieutenant in the British Army, was highly critical of Britain's military commanders

Haig believed that the war could only be won on the Western Front. This caused friction with Lloyd George, who disagreed with this strategy, and who intrigued against Haig....

BBC History website

Now it's your turn

1 Why do you think so many men died during the Battle of the Somme?
2 Some of these accounts are written with hindsight. Does this make them more, or less, reliable?
3 Charles Hudson argues that 'huge bombardments failed again and again.' Does this mean Haig had not learned the lessons of earlier fighting in the war?

Extension work

Does Haig deserve to be known as 'Butcher of the Somme?'

Check your progress

I can explain why the Battle of the Somme failed.
I can explain why so many soldiers died.
I can understand why some people think Haig was the 'Butcher of the Somme'.

Casualties: soldiers killed or wounded in battle
Intrigued: tried to undermine or remove

'A black day for the German army!'

Objectives

By the end of this lesson you will be able to:

- explore reasons for the success of the British Army in 1918
- explore reasons for Haig being known as the 'general who won World War One'

In December 1917 Russia stopped fighting, giving Germany an opportunity to achieve victory on the Western Front before new American troops arrived in the summer of 1918. Ludendorf, the leader of the German army, launched an offensive in March 1918 and nearly made the breakthrough.

Getting you thinking

The Ludendorf Offensive shocked the Allies, forcing them to plan and fight together. They united their armies under the French General Foch, as supreme commander of the Allied Forces. They managed to stop the Germans just short of Paris, on the River Marne – almost the same place they had stopped the German armies in September 1914. After careful planning and preparation they

The Ypres battlefield on the Western Front

Allied Naval Blockade: blocking off Germany's ports to prevent it importing food or raw materials for the war effort

attacked the Germans at the Battle of Amiens, on 8 August 1918, which Ludendorf called 'a black day for the German Army'. He later said that he realised on that day that Germany could not win the war.

What had changed?

The Allies developed what became known as the 'all-arms attack.'

- Smoke was used to obscure the battlefield and protect the infantry who were equipped with light machine guns and rifle grenades. They were expected to move fast. If they came upon a German strongpoint they were ordered to go round it, not attack it head on.
- Next came the heavy machine guns. Behind these, the mortars.
- Then the tanks, used to destroy any remaining barbed wire or other obstacles.
- Flying above were aircraft, guiding the infantry and tanks, letting the artillery know targets, shooting or bombing the Germans themselves whenever possible.
- Artillery provided a creeping barrage, moving slowly forward, just ahead of the British infantry and preventing Germans from shooting at the advancing troops.
- They also delivered poisonous gas shells.
- Next came supply tanks, bringing up ammunition and reinforcements in order to keep the attack moving. This was all carefully co-ordinated.
- It was a war of movement – and it worked. Over 400,000 prisoners were taken, and 7,000 heavy guns captured in a few days. The frontline around Ypres moved forward 13 kilometres in a single day.

Germany found it hard to replace lost men and supplies. People were starving due to the *Allied Naval Blockade*; 1916–1917 was known as the 'turnip winter' because that was all there was to eat. Opposition to the war mounted. Ludendorf asked the *Kaiser* to choose a new government, led by civilians, that could negotiate an end to the war.

Now it's your turn

1 How was the 'all-arms attack' different from the tactics used on the Somme in 1916?
2 Does the success at Amiens and after prove that Haig had learned his lesson from the failures in 1915, 1916 and 1917?
3 Do the events of 1918 alter your opinion of General Haig as a World War One leader?

Check your progress

I can understand why the Allies broke through the German lines in August 1918.

I can understand the difference in tactics used in 1918 and the part that this played in preventing a repeat of the Somme.

I can re-assess my opinion of Haig following the events of 1918.

Kaiser: emperor of Germany

Armistice

Objectives

By the end of this lesson you will be able to:

- explore the reactions of individuals at the end of the war
- decide if the Allies won the war or Germany lost it

At 11 o'clock, on 11 November 1918 the guns fell silent all along the Western Front. The war finally stopped everywhere. An *armistice* had been signed that morning. It seemed there was to be no more killing.

Germany's allies had left the war – on 29 September Bulgaria surrendered, on 30 October the Ottomans and then, on 3 November, Austria-Hungary. Germany was left to fight alone. All the military and economic might of the Allies was directed against Germany.

Germany expected the peace to be negotiated around President Wilson's *14 Points*. They anticipated a 'just and fair peace'.

Getting you thinking

Armistice, 11 November, 1918. The leader of the Allied forces, Marshal Foche, second from right, is carrying the text of the armistice agreement signed by Germany

Why did the war end?

BLOCKADE: Germany could not get essential supplies to make weapons and it desperately needed imported food.

ATTRITION: Both sides had HUGE casualties, but Germany had fewer men to lose. The arrival of America DID NOT win the war, it just made it end a bit quicker.

NEW WEAPONS such as the tank provided mobile fire support.

NEW TACTICS which combined artillery, troops, fire support, teamwork, tanks, aerial reconnaissance.

Answer to the question 'Why did World War One end?' from the website 'Yahoo! Answers'

Do you agree with this answer? Is it a full explanation, or a partial explanation? What else do you need to know?

Armistice: *agreement to stop fighting*
14 Points: *set of proposals put forward by the US president as a basis for ending the war*

Why couldn't Germany continue fighting? German troops were, after all, still in France and Belgium and there was no fighting inside Germany. However support for the war inside Germany was fading, as the effects of the Allied blockade were increasingly felt. The political will to carry on the war vanished; strikes spread, along with the demand for a new democratic government, and there were *mutinies* in the army and navy.

The Allies made the following demands for a ceasefire:

- removal of the Kaiser
- withdrawal from France and Belgium
- surrender of all weapons
- release of all prisoners of war
- surrender of all U-boats and warships

In return, Allied troops would not enter Germany.

Very reluctantly, the Germans agreed.

When the news reached London, crowds rapidly appeared on the streets, shouting and cheering with delight. The Daily Mirror called it 'the greatest, gladdest, most wonderful day in British history,' and reported that 'London went wild with delight.'

From 'Peace and War' by Philip A Sauvain

In the trenches the response was rather different:

When we'd nearly finished the food I said to them casually, 'The war's over at 11 o'clock this morning.' Somebody said, 'Yeah?' Somebody else said, 'Go on!' They just went on eating ... we were so war weary that we were just ready to accept whatever came...

Corporal Pankhurst writing home

Now it's your turn

1 How do you explain the different reactions in London and in the trenches to the ending of the war?
2 Make a list of all the reasons the war ended. Split your list into two, as shown here:

Allied victory	German defeat

Check your progress

I can describe people's reactions at the end of the war.
I can suggest why people might have reacted in different ways.
I can make a convincing argument about the reasons for the end of the war.

Mutinies: soldiers and sailors refusing to obey orders

Was it all worth it?

Objectives

By the end of this lesson you will be able to:

- explore the cost of the war
- try to decide if it was worth it

About 20 million soldiers were wounded, gassed or *maimed* during World War One. Over eight million civilians were massacred or died of starvation or disease. Another six million died from the *pandemic* of Spanish Flu at the end of the war.

Four empires – Germany, Austria-Hungary, Russia and the Ottomans – collapsed, to be replaced by a host of newly independent countries.

In France, over nine thousand square miles of agricultural land were destroyed. It was the same story wherever the war was fought; 12 million tons of shipping had been sunk, mostly by U-boats. Was it worth it?

Getting you thinking

Nearly 65 million men fought in World War One and around 10 million soldiers were killed. Fighting took place on the Western Front; on the Eastern Front with Russia; on the Italian border with Austria-Hungary; in the Balkans; against the Ottoman Empire in Gallipoli and the Middle East; in Africa, in Asia and the Pacific; and there were naval clashes in most of the oceans around the world. It really was a world war.

The money spent was staggering:

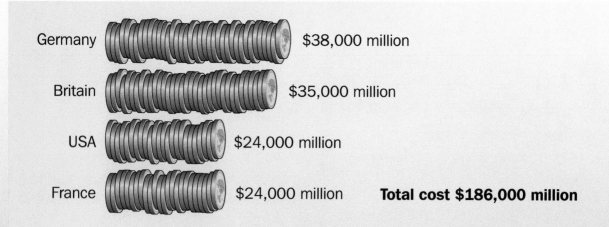

Germany — $38,000 million

Britain — $35,000 million

USA — $24,000 million

France — $24,000 million   **Total cost $186,000 million**

Most of this was paid for by taxes, although people bought 'war bonds' with their savings, to be paid back after the war. Most governments were faced with huge debts to repay once the war ended.

The total number of dead for the British Empire is given as 998,000. But where did these soldiers come from?

Maimed: lost one or more of limbs *Pandemic: major outbreak of disease*
Demobilised: let out of the army

Nearly one in three war deaths were from the countries of the empire. Why were these men fighting for Britain?

What happened when the troops came home and were *demobilised*?

And what about all those families where men – fathers, brothers, sons – didn't come home? How would they survive? How would all those women who had given so much to the war effort find a husband with so many men dead? And what would happen to all those factories making shells, tanks and uniforms?

Although I was an expert machine-gunner, I was a *numbskull* so far as any trade or craft was concerned. Lloyd George had been full of big talk about making a country fit for heroes to live in, but it was just so much hot air. I joined the queues for jobs as messengers, window cleaners and *scullions*. It was a complete let-down for thousands like me ... there were no jobs for the 'heroes' who hung around the billiard halls as I did. The government never kept their promise...

George Coppard, 'With a machine-gun to Cambrai' (1969)

Now it's your turn

1 What did Britain hope to achieve by going to war? Did it achieve its aims?
2 Was it worth the cost?
3 Do you think Britain could have become a 'land fit for heroes' in 1918? Give reasons for your answer.

Check your progress

I can describe how much World War One cost Britain.
I can suggest some of the impacts that the war had on Britain.
I can make a reasoned judgement about the impact of the war.

NIGERIA 5,000 DEATHS

SIERRA LEONE 1,000 DEATHS

UGANDA 1,500 DEATHS

ZAMBIA 2,000 DEATHS

CHINESE LABOUR CORPS 2,000 DEATHS

GHANA 1,200 DEATHS

KENYA 2,000 DEATHS

MALAWI 3,000 DEATHS

NEW ZEALAND 16,000 DEATHS

SOUTH AFRICA 7,000 DEATHS

NEWFOUNDLAND 1,000 DEATHS

WEST INDIES 500 DEATHS

GREAT BRITAIN (INCL. IRELAND) 761,000 DEATHS

INDIA 62,000 DEATHS

AUSTRALIA 59,000 DEATHS

CANADA 57,000 DEATHS

Note: Former British colonies are listed by their current names.

Numbskull: *stupid, with no skills*
Scullion: *servant doing the worst tasks in the kitchen*

Changes to the map of Europe

Objectives

By the end of this lesson you will be able to:

- explore the changes to the map of Europe brought about by the war
- try to decide if the world was a safer place in 1919 than in 1914

Four of the six great empires that started the war – Germany, Austria-Hungary, Russia and the Ottomans – had disappeared from the map of Europe, to be replaced by a host of newly *independent* countries. Nationalism had triumphed. Many people now had, as they wished for in 1914, their own countries to live in: remember those people in Bosnia who wanted to join Serbia, and not be ruled by Austria-Hungary? Would this make peace more likely or less likely in the future?

Europe in 1919 (pre-1914 borders shown in dark red – see map on page 20)

Nationalities: people with a common historical background and identity
Independent: not being ruled by another country

Getting you thinking

Austria–Hungary went to war to keep its empire safe. It was worried that the *nationalities* within its borders – such as the Poles, Czechs, Serbs, Bosnians – wanted their *independence*. The same was true for the Ottoman Empire – all the nationalities in the Balkans and North Africa and the Middle East wanted their independence too. As these empires were losing the war, each group of people took the opportunity to declare their independence and set up their own country, creating all the new countries on the map.

When the winning countries – Britain, France, the USA and Italy – met in Versailles in 1919 to draw up the peace treaty with Germany, all these new countries were there too, demanding that their independence be recognised by the Great Powers. In effect, these countries already existed – they had set themselves up, they had governments, armies, political parties – but they needed international recognition to make it legal.

President Wilson's 14 points (see page 42) had included the idea of self-determination – the idea that each nationality should run its own affairs. There would be no more colonies or empires. That way, he argued, there would be no more wars, because wars started when countries wanted their freedom. The *Great Powers* were happy, therefore, to let all these small countries exist. It would, Wilson argued, make the world safer. It would also, Britain and France argued, make the losing countries – Germany, Austria, the Ottoman Empire – weaker, so they would not be able to fight any more.

It could also be argued that lots of small countries might make war more likely, not less; there are simply more countries to quarrel with each other. The alliance system (see page 22) between the powerful countries before World War One was meant to keep the peace by balancing one group of powers against another – and that had failed.

Now it's your turn APP

1 Which empires survived the war?
2 List all the new countries on the map of Europe. Which empires were they made from?
3 In 1914 the Black Hand Gang assassinated Franz Ferdinand because it wanted Bosnia to be part of Serbia. Did the gang get its way?
4 In 1914 France wanted Alsace-Lorraine back from Germany. Did this happen?
5 After 1919 all the Czechs lived in Czechoslovakia, all the Poles in Poland and all the Finns in Finland. Do you think this made peace easier to keep?

Check your progress

I can see how the map of Europe changed between 1914 and 1919.

I can understand why it changed between 1914 and 1919.

I can discuss whether or not the changes made war less likely in the future.

Great Powers: in 1919 these were Britain, France, Germany and the USA

'The war to end all wars?'

It is often said that the generals – and the politicians for that matter – usually prepare to fight the last war, not the next one. That is clearly what happened with World War One. Everyone expected the war to be over by Christmas, that it would be a jolly adventure, a war of movement, and that the cavalry would race across the battlefield and capture the Germans.

Getting you thinking

There hadn't been a major war in Europe since the Franco–Prussian War of 1870-71. All the recent wars had been *colonial* wars, against poorly armed native troops. That is where most of the generals had learned their job, but it was very different from controlling millions of men on the Western Front.

Perhaps this explains the British Army's failures in 1914 and 1915, and General Haig's failures in 1916 and 1917. Technology had advanced and defences were now much stronger than attackers. New weapons controlled the battlefield, and it took a long time – and lots of

A tank beside a road on the Western Front in World War One

Colony: one country owned or controlled by a bigger more powerful one

casualties – before the generals learned their lessons. But eventually they did. In 1918 both the Germans – in the spring, and the Allies – in the summer and autumn, managed to break through the trenches and push back the enemy. Careful planning and co-ordination of all parts of the army meant it became possible to break out of the stalemate in the trenches and push on for victory. The war became a war of movement, victory and resources.

Just what was the impact of the war? How did it affect Britain, and British society? Millions of men had fought in the war, and millions of women had done men's jobs so that they could fight. Industry had been affected, focusing on the production of shells, weapons and uniforms etc, rather than consumer goods for people to buy. Agriculture had been affected – much more food had to be grown at home, because of the German U-boats. Finance had been affected – the war had cost Britain in the region of $35,000 million and much of that still needed to be paid for. The British Empire had been involved too – around 250,000 empire soldiers lost their lives in the war. What was done well and what could have been done better?

In this unit you have looked at World War One. Now it is time to try and draw some conclusions from your study.

Assessment task

It is 1920. The war is over. The peace treaties have been signed. The world is getting back to normal. It is now time to try to learn the lessons of World War One. You have been asked by the government to prepare a report on the war, so that the military can plan more effectively for any future conflict.

What will your report focus on? What should it contain? How are you going to present the finished report?

Check your level

I can describe the way in which World War One battles were fought, and suggest my own enquiry questions:

'What do I already know about World War One? What else do I want to know? What questions do I still need to ask?'

Level **5**

I can carry out an historical enquiry into the way in which World War One battles were fought, using and refining my own enquiry questions:

'That question doesn't really give me the answer I expected – do I need to ask a different question?'

Level **6**

I can carry out my own historical enquiry into the way in which World War One battles were fought by defining, and refining, enquiry questions and evaluating the process:

'That question doesn't really give me the answer I expected. Do I need to change my question, or do I need to do some more research? I could have done that better if I had…'

Level **7**

2

From boom to bust

Sometimes historians examine an event in depth. We can have whole books on one person or on a single year. At other times it is important for historians to be able to sum up bigger periods of history in a page. This is an important skill; it is sometimes called 'big picture' history. Summing up a period of history does not always have to be in writing. Sometimes we might choose an object to sum up an era. The image chosen here sums up the period you are about to study, the 1920s and 1930s. It shows a factory warehouse full of cars, the Model T Ford, ready for delivery to the car dealers who will sell them.

Questions

1 What does this choice of image suggest to you about the period of the 1920s and 1930s?

2 How would you create a 'big picture' summary of the first decade of the 21st century? Which object or person do you think best represents this period? Explain your choice in writing.

What makes a great power?

Objectives

By the end of this lesson you will be able to:

- give examples of the features of a great power
- explain how the features of a great power changed over time

Throughout history some nations have been more powerful than others; for example, the Romans, the Mongols and the Aztecs. In this lesson, we will consider what made a great power in the 20th century and beyond by examining two countries: the United Kingdom and China.

Getting you thinking

Which country do you think is the most powerful today? What makes this country so powerful?

Great powers in 1919

Britain

In 1919 Britain controlled a huge empire that included India, Australia, and South Africa. Britain's empire extended to every continent. This empire was protected by the Royal Navy, which was the most powerful navy in the world. The navy continued to develop between 1919 and 1939.

After the 1919 Treaty of Versailles, the League of Nations was established to help avoid future wars. The first secretary of the organisation was Eric Drummond, who was British. Britain had been the first country to industrialise, but in the 20th century other countries began to develop at a faster rate. The British economy, like many others, suffered in the late 1920s and 1930s.

China

This is the flag of the old Chinese Republic, before the communists took power. By 1919 China was no longer an empire; it had removed its emperor in 1911. The Treaty of Versailles gave the Japanese control over Germany's Chinese territory, causing great anger in China. China did not join the League of Nations.

At the time, China was largely a rural, *subsistence economy*. The Chinese national government had little power. China was divided into areas each ruled by a general or warlord. Some people in China began to look to *communism* as a way to organise their country. Meanwhile, various foreign powers had special rights in China. Britain, for example, controlled a part of the country called Hong Kong, while Portugal controlled Macau.

Subsistence economy: an economy in which people grow enough food to feed only themselves

Great powers in the 21st century

Britain

The British Empire was *dismantled* in the 20th century; countries like India and South Africa gained their independence. The empire was replaced with an organisation, headed by the Queen, called the Commonwealth.

Today Britain is a nuclear power. The British armed services serve in conflicts across the world and Britain is part of NATO, the North Atlantic Treaty Organisation, a military alliance based in Western Europe and North America.

The British economy has lost most of its manufacturing base and is much more reliant on service industries like banking. Britain is a member of the United Nations and has a permanent seat on its Security Council, the body tasked with keeping world peace.

China

This is China's present-day flag. China expanded in the second half of the 20th century. This was as a result of military intervention in Tibet, and the return of territories such as Hong Kong and Macau from Western powers.

China is ruled by a communist government. It is also a nuclear power, a member of the United Nations and one of the five powers with permanent seats on the security council.

China's economy industrialised rapidly in the second half of the 20th century and it is now one of the three wealthiest countries in the world. China is home to more than one billion of the world's population.

A seaplane flies over British warships of the Royal Navy during World War One

Communism: a political system developed from Karl Marx's ideas
Dismantled: taken to pieces

Boom: How strong was the US economy in the 1920s?

The United States of America increased its power after World War One. It emerged as the most important economy in the world in the 1920s. Let's examine the features of economic growth in the USA.

Getting you thinking

Examine the photograph. What is happening in this picture? Where do you think this photograph was taken? What kind of people are in the picture? What are they doing?

Making the bodies for Model T Fords, 1915

During World War One, the American economy grew enormously as the US built factories to supply weapons, equipment and uniforms. At the end of the war there were concerns that this prosperity could end, so the US government put in place measures to try to protect the economy.

In the 1920s the US placed high *tariffs* on imported goods, making them expensive for US citizens to buy. Unemployment was low and so was inflation. There was an enormous increase in consumer goods. Cars, radios, telephones and ready-made clothes were all affordable for ordinary workers. They could either pay for them with cash or use a new system, hire purchase, which spread the cost of an expensive item over months or years.

The photograph on the opposite page is of the Ford Motor Company in Detroit. It shows workers on a production line making Model T cars. Ford became one of the most successful companies in the world by producing cheaper cars. They did this by employing people to work doing only one small job on each car. This meant workers did not have to be as skilled and therefore did not have to be paid so highly; the price of cars fell from an average of $850 in 1905 to $290 in 1925.

Another important feature of the US economy was the growth of the stock market. Many people bought stocks and shares in companies such as Ford and watched as their value increased seemingly without end. It seemed an easy way to make money and many ordinary Americans began investing in the market using a system a bit like hire purchase, called 'buying on margin'. This involved having the money only for a percentage of the stocks you wanted (sometimes as little as 10 per cent) and borrowing the rest from your stockbroker. For example, if you bought $100 dollars worth of stock, you only had to have $50 or less in your pocket; the rest was borrowed. If the stock rose to $150 you could sell it, pay back the $50 dollars you had borrowed from your stock broker and make $50 for yourself. The problem came if the price of the stock fell; then you had to find money to pay back the broker. The market kept rising, however, and this encouraged more and more people to buy and to keep spending more money than they actually had.

Now it's your turn

Here are some of the factors that enabled the US economy to grow in the 1920s. Explain how each of them helped.
- World War One
- tariffs
- mass production
- hire purchase/buying on margin
- cheap goods

Check your progress

⭐ I can explain some causes of economic growth in the USA.
⭐⭐ I can show how each factor helped the economy to grow.
⭐⭐⭐ I can identify some problems with economic growth in the 1920s.

Tariffs: taxes placed on goods that are made outside the country

1920s USA: the 'melting pot'

Since the colonisation of the USA by Europeans in the 16th century, many different nationalities had become US citizens. In the 1920s the issue of immigration became very important in American politics. This section will examine why and what the effect of this was.

Getting you thinking

Slavery ended in the USA in 1865. Almost immediately an organisation called the Ku Klux Klan (KKK) was established in the southern states to stop African Americans from getting the vote. They also opposed immigration into the USA. Look at the photograph of the Klan members. Why do you think they might have dressed like that?

The KKK

The KKK grew rapidly during the 1920s. By 1925 there were over four million members, including people elected to run the country. They used violence and intimidation to get what they wanted.

Members of the Ku Klux Klan in the woods near Atlanta, Georgia, 1921

Disembarked: brought ashore from a ship
Tenements: low-rental apartment buildings, often of poor quality

A lad whipped with branches until his back was ribboned flesh: a Negress beaten and left helpless to contract pneumonia from exposure dies; a white girl, divorcee, beaten into unconsciousness in her home; a naturalized foreigner flogged until his back was pulp because he married an American woman; a Negro lashed until he sold his land to a white man for a fraction of its value.

R. A. Patton, writing about the activities of the Ku Klux Klan in 1929

What can we learn about the Klan's beliefs from this source?

Immigration control

Between 1900 and 1920, 14 million immigrants arrived in the USA. After World War One, the US passed a series of laws designed to limit immigration. They adopted a quota system; the biggest quotas were given to white Anglo-Saxon countries (about two thirds of the total allowed). No African country could send more than 100 people, but 34,007 could come from England. Only 3,845 could come from Italy, but 51,227 from Germany; only 2,248 were allowed from Russia, but 28,567 from Ireland. Can you think why the quotas were set the way they were?

Life as an immigrant

Many of the immigrants that arrived in the USA between 1892 and 1954 took their first steps on American soil at the immigration processing centre on Ellis Island in New York. Passengers in first and second class had their papers checked on board, but the poorer passengers were *disembarked* and checked for their legal status and for diseases.

Once in the USA, many people initially settled in New York. It was the centre for the ready-made clothing industry and many immigrants worked long hours in the garment trade. Houses called *tenements* were common; overcrowding and poor sanitation helped make tuberculosis one of the main causes of death in the early 20th century.

Sacco and Vanzetti

In 1920 the Federal Bureau of Investigation (FBI) arrested an Italian-American *political agitator*, Andrea Salsedo. After eight weeks Salsedo's body was found on the pavement outside the building he was being held in; the FBI claimed he had committed suicide. Two of his friends, Sacco and Vanzetti, began carrying guns. They were arrested and accused of armed robbery and murder. They were found guilty and held for seven years while people appealed for their retrial, claiming they were innocent. In August 1927 they were *executed*.

Now it's your turn

Were the 1920s a good time for all Americans? Explain your answer.

Check your progress

I can begin to explore the experience of minorities in the USA.

I can begin to compare the experience of minorities with those of white Americans.

I can decide, based on what I've learnt, whether or not the treatment of minorities was fair.

Political agitator: someone who stirs up public feeling about issues
Executed: put to death

What can Harlem tell us about America between the wars?

Objectives

By the end of this lesson you will be able to:

- build a picture of life in Harlem using evidence
- make a judgement about what this may tell you about life in the wider USA

Harlem is a part of New York. After the end of slavery in the 19th century, African Americans began to move north to places like New York in increasing numbers. Harlem became a predominantly black area of New York. This section will examine what Harlem can tell us about life in the USA between the wars.

Getting you thinking

Examine Source 1. What suggestions can you make about Harlem by using just the photograph as evidence?

In 1925 a white university professor, Alain Locke, published a book, 'The New Negro: An Interpretation'. Locke's book was a collection of poems, essays and other writings by African American writers.

Harlem became a centre of jazz and blues music. Clubs like the Cotton Club and theatres like the Apollo attracted musicians from all over America. Black stars like Duke Ellington, Bessie Smith, and Cab Calloway got sell-out crowds, which included large numbers of white Americans. During *prohibition*, many *speakeasies* were set up for illegal drinking.

Here in Manhattan is not merely the largest Negro community in the world, but the first concentration in history of so many diverse elements of Negro life. It has attracted the African, the West Indian, the Negro American; has brought together the Negro of the North and the Negro of the South; the man from the city and the man from the town and village; the peasant, the student, the business man, the professional man, artist, poet, musician, adventurer and worker, preacher and criminal, exploiter and social outcast. Each group has come with its own separate motives and for its own special ends, but their greatest experience has been the finding of one another.

Source 2 *Alain Locke (1925)*

Nor did ordinary Negroes like the growing influx of whites toward Harlem after sundown, flooding the little cabarets and bars where formerly only colored people laughed and sang, and where now the strangers were given the best ringside tables to sit and stare at the Negro customers – like amusing animals in a zoo. The Negroes said: 'We can't go downtown and sit and stare at you in your clubs. You won't even let us in your clubs.'

Source 3 *Langston Hughes (1940)*

Prohibition: the banning of the production and sale of alcohol in the USA
Speakeasies: illegal drinking clubs set up during prohibition

Source 1 *The Cotton Club in Harlem, New York, 1930s*

Harlem was overcrowded and expensive. In the 1930s, there were 233 people per acre in comparison with 133 for the rest of Manhattan. Rents were more expensive for black tenants than for white tenants. In 1932 twice as many patients died in Harlem Hospital than in Bellevue Hospital, a white area of New York. About half of the married women in Harlem worked as servants in the rest of the city; they often waited on corners to be hired each day.

The women arrive as early as eight a.m. and remain as late as one p.m. or until they are hired. In rain or shine, hot or cold, they wait to work for ten, fifteen, and twenty cents per hour.

Source 4 *'The Crisis Magazine', Ella Barker and Marvel Cooke (1935)*

Now it's your turn

1 Use all the evidence on the page to describe life in Harlem.
2 Do you think Harlem was a typical place? What hypotheses could you make about life for African Americans elsewhere in the USA?

Check your progress

I can use evidence to describe life in Harlem.

I can draw conclusions about life in Harlem from the evidence.

I can draw conclusions about the rest of the USA using the sources on Harlem.

Who was the most significant African American of the 1920s and 1930s?

Significance is a way to consider why something is important. In this section we will look at several people and you will decide how significant they are.

Getting you thinking

There are different ways of thinking about someone's significance. The historian Geoffrey Partington (1980) suggested using the following *criteria*:

- Were they important to people living at the time?
- Did they affect people's lives a lot?
- Did they affect a lot of people's lives?
- Did they change things for a long time?
- Do they still affect us today?

How do Nelson Mandela and David Beckham measure up with these criteria?

Jesse Owens

Jesse Owens was born into poverty in 1913. The son of a Southern *sharecropper* and the grandson of a slave, he became the fastest man on the planet. Owens won four gold medals at the 1936 Olympics in Berlin, undermining Hitler's claim that whites were the superior race. In those days, all Olympic athletes were amateurs and had to work for a living; Owens spent much of the rest of his life working with underprivileged children. He was awarded the USA Medal of Freedom in 1976, and died in 1980. Today the Jesse Owens Foundation supports underprivileged young people.

Jesse Owens at the start of his record-breaking 200 metres race, 1936 Olympics, Berlin, Germany

Criteria: standards by which something can be judged

Bessie Coleman

Bessie Coleman was born in 1892. Before she was ten years old, her father left the family and Bessie's mother had to become a servant, leaving Bessie to bring up her younger sisters. Bessie completed school and spent one year at university before her savings ran out and she was forced to return home to work as a laundress. In 1915 she moved to Chicago and became a manicurist. By the age of 27 Bessie was determined to amount to something; she wanted to become a pilot. In 1920 Bessie set off for France to learn to fly. She became the first qualified black female pilot. Between 1922 and 1925 Bessie was flying in shows all over America, trying to raise enough money to set up her own flying school. In 1926, however, Bessie fell to her death, as her mechanic lost control of the plane. Ten thousand people filed past her coffin and thousands more attended her funeral. In 1992, the USA put Bessie's image on a postage stamp.

Paul Robeson

Paul Robeson was born in 1892. The son of a former slave, he became one of the most famous singers in the 20th century. Paul's mother died and at the age of 12 he was working as a kitchen boy. He won a scholarship to university in 1915, where he excelled in all sports. He was often dropped, however, as some teams refused to play against black sportspeople. Robeson qualified as a lawyer in 1923 but decided to become a singer. He campaigned for civil rights and travelled all over the world, performing with the biggest stars of the day. Robeson campaigned against fascism but his politics were unpopular in the USA, and after World War Two he was accused of being a communist. His passport was taken from him and he found himself unable to earn a living. He moved to Europe where he eventually died.

Now it's your turn

1 Which person do you think people living in their time would have thought was significant, both in the USA and outside the USA?
2 Which person do you think people alive today find most significant?

Check your progress

☆   I can give reasons why I think a person might be significant to an historian.
☆☆   I can use Partington's rules to decide whether or not a person is significant.
☆☆☆   I can devise my own rules to decide whether or not a person is significant.

Sharecropper: a farmer who rented the land he farmed by giving the landowner a share of the crop as payment

The Depression

The collapse of the American economy, known as the Depression, had consequences not only for Americans but also for much of the rest of the world. This section examines some of those consequences.

Objectives

By the end of this lesson you will be able to:

- describe the consequences of the Depression
- examine the importance of those consequences

Getting you thinking

Below are the lyrics of a popular song from 1931. What information about the consequences of the crash does this song give us?

> They used to tell me I was building a dream, and so I followed the mob,
> When there was earth to plough, or guns to bear, I was always there right
>   on the job.
> They used to tell me I was building a dream, with peace and glory ahead,
> Why should I be standing in line, just waiting for bread?
>
> Once I built a railroad, I made it run, made it race against time.
> Once I built a railroad; now it's done. Brother, can you spare a dime?
> Once I built a tower, up to the sun, brick, and rivet, and lime;
> Once I built a tower, now it's done. Brother, can you spare a dime?
>
> Once in khaki suits, gee we looked swell,
> Full of that Yankee Doodly Dum,
> Half a million boots went slogging through Hell,
> And I was the kid with the drum!
>
> Say, don't you remember, they called me Al; it was Al all the time.
> Why don't you remember, I'm your pal? Buddy, can you spare a dime?

'Brother, Can You Spare a Dime', lyrics by Yip Harburg, music by Jay Gorney (1931)

Effects on the USA

One of the most immediate effects was a collapse in the value of goods produced. Production fell by more than $40 billion and factories and shops were forced to close. Millions of people became unemployed; some of them marched on Washington D.C. where they set up camps called Hoovervilles, named after the US president Herbert Clark Hoover.

What can the photograph on the opposite page tell us about life in the Hoovervilles?

In 1933 Hoover lost the election and President Franklin Delano Roosevelt took office promising a 'new deal for the American people'.

'Hoovervilles', named after US President Hoover, were shanty towns that appeared on the edges of American cities during the Depression

Effects on Britain

As the US economy collapsed, so too did American demand for foreign goods. Unemployment grew rapidly in Britain, doubling from 1,434,000 in January 1929 to 2,979,000 by January 1933. For the first time the Labour Party became the biggest party in parliament, forming a government in 1929. In September 1931 there was a naval mutiny at Invergordon over pay cuts.

Effects on Germany

The Americans had lent money to Germany to help it recover after economic collapse in 1924. Now they wanted the money back. German banks went bust and millions of savers lost everything; industry collapsed as businesses were forced to pay back money they had borrowed. This was the second collapse of the Germany economy in five years. The Nazi party – which had been marginalised until this point – began to get many more votes as people looked for new solutions.

Now it's your turn

1 Make a list of all of the consequences of the Depression.
2 Which are the three most important consequences you have found? Explain your answer.

Check your progress

I can describe some of the consequences of the Depression.
I can decide which consequences were the most important.
I can explain why I think these consequences were the most important.

Why did the US economy collapse?

Objectives

By the end of this lesson you will be able to:

- judge the relative importance of the causes of the Depression
- identify the consequences of the Depression

In 1929 the US stock market crashed, heralding the end of the *boom* and tipping the western world economies into a crisis and depression. Why did this happen and what were the consequences?

Getting you thinking

Why do you think gold is so expensive? Why do Premier League footballers earn so much? This is connected to supply (how much there is of a good or skill) and demand (how much people want something). When there is low supply and high demand, prices are high; when supply is high but demand is low, prices are low. Can you think of two more examples of goods or skills that are expensive because the supply is low and the demand is high?

Why did the economy collapse?

Supply and demand

Tariffs had helped US consumer goods industries develop, but supply soon outstripped demand. People did not buy more telephones once they had one, so workers were laid off. The unemployed couldn't afford to buy more goods, so demand decreased. This led to more workers losing their jobs, and so on, in a downward spiral.

The stock market collapse

In October 1929 some big investors began to sell their stock. This led to a crisis of confidence in the stock market and caused panic selling by many people. The price of stocks and shares collapsed. Many people found themselves owing vast sums of money to brokers because they had bought shares on margin (see p. 55). Thousands went bankrupt, banks closed and stocks became worthless.

Farming

Farmers had never benefited from the boom. Food prices fell, but machinery was expensive and it put farm workers out of a job. Over-farming and a drought in the 1930s in the Central Plains turned the land into a *dustbowl*.

Credit

People who bought goods on credit found that when they became unemployed, they were unable to pay back the money they owed. This led to more businesses failing, thus increasing unemployment.

Boom: time of economic prosperity

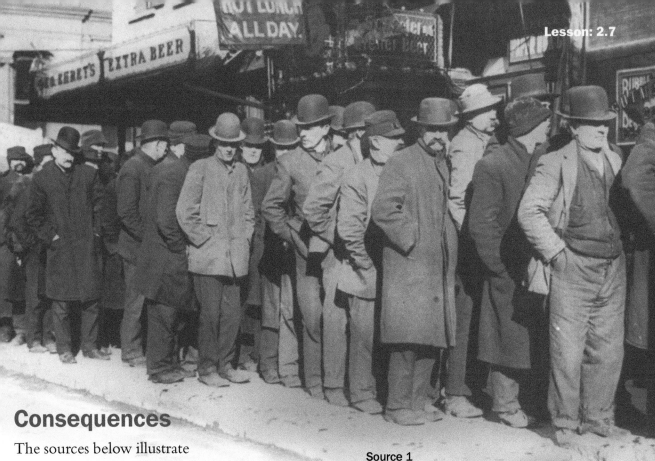

Consequences

The sources below illustrate some of the consequences of the depression.

Source 1
Breadline: Unemployed workers in New York City

You know my condition is bad. I used to get a pension from the government and that stopped. It is now nearly seven months I am out of work ... I have four children who are in need of clothes and food ... my daughter who is eight is very ill and not recovering. My rent is due in two months and I am afraid of being put out.

Source 2 *Letter from a tenement dweller in Harlem to a congressman*

The long drought that ruined hundreds of Arkansas farms last summer had a dramatic sequel today when some 500 farmers, most of them white men and some of them armed, marched on the business section of this town shouting they must have food for themselves and their families. The invaders announced their intention to take it from the stores unless it were provided from some other source without cost.

Source 3 *Newspaper report, 3 January 1931*

Now it's your turn

1 What is the most important cause of the Depression? Give each one a mark out of 10 for importance and explain your score.
2 Use the sources to create a newspaper article about the effects of the Depression on the American people. Your newspaper should be from the time.

Check your progress

I can describe the causes and consequences of the Depression.
I can use source material to write a newspaper article.
I can decide which cause had the most impact, and can explain my choice.

Dustbowl: a desert-like region, where food cannot be grown

Russia: rulers and revolutions!

Objectives

By the end of this lesson you will be able to:

- comment upon Nicholas as a ruler
- analyse his impact on history

One of the key questions about the past is how much one individual can shape history. In this section we will examine Tsar Nicholas II of Russia and think about the impact he had upon history.

Getting you thinking

Examine the picture showing the coronation of Tsar Nicholas II. What does it suggest about:

- Russia in the 19th century? Can you find clues about religion, the military and art?
- the role of the Tsar?

Nicholas II was born in 1868, the son of Alexander III. Upon his father's death in 1894 he became Tsar, with as much power as medieval English kings. The Tsarina was Princess Alexandra. They had five children but their son was to suffer from the disease *haemophilia*.

The Coronation of Tsar Nicholas II

Haemophilia: a disease that prevents blood from clotting

Nicholas tried to rule Russia alone. He did not trust his ministers and wanted to keep all the powers of the Tsar. He also wanted Russia to be powerful. As other countries expanded their empire, so did Nicholas, looking to the east and Manchuria. This led to war with Japan in 1904, a war that Russia lost. Nicholas was blamed.

In January 1905, marchers advanced upon the Winter Palace in St Petersburg to demand change. Troops opened fire and more than 100 people were killed. Unrest spread and by October the Tsar was forced to give in to demands for change and promise a parliament.

> *Our souls are fighting for the right against the evil. You are proving yourself the Autocrat without which Russia cannot exist. God anointed you in your coronation and God, who is always near you, will save your country and throne through your firmness.*
>
> Tsarina Alexandra writing to her husband, 1915

The Russian *Duma* met and more people had a voice in the running of Russia. Radicals, however, were banned from voting, and the Tsar's secret police continued to crush any opposition. Nicholas believed that although some in Russia disliked him, the peasants loved him. He and the Tsarina spent much of the time living in their country palace. In 1913 Nicholas celebrated the 300th anniversary of Romanov rule.

In 1914, World War One broke out. Nicholas made the decision to mobilise his army along the border with Germany; the Germans saw this as an act of aggression and declared war. Nicholas commanded Russia's military and civilian efforts; he ignored much advice and soon there was a lack of supplies for both the military and the civilian population. His most constant source of advice was the Tsarina and a Russian monk Rasputin, who had gained influence with the royal couple because of his ability to treat their son's disease. Many people hated Rasputin and he was murdered in 1916. By 1917 revolution had broken out in Russia and Nicholas had abdicated; in July 1918 he and his family were shot.

Now it's your turn

1 What strengths and weaknesses did Nicholas have as a ruler?
2 Was it inevitable that Nicholas would lose power?
3 Do you think he was to blame for this? Were there any points when he could have done things differently?

Check your progress

★ I can describe what Nicholas was like as a ruler.
★★ I can say how much to blame Nicholas was for his problems.
★★★ I can identify which problems were beyond Nicholas's control.

Duma: the Russian parliament

Changing Russia: the beginnings of communism

Objectives

By the end of this lesson you will be able to:

- describe what communism means
- explain Lenin's role in the development of communism

Much of the history of the 20th century has been concerned with the struggle between two systems for running a country: capitalism and communism. This lesson examines communist ideas and the life of Vladimir Lenin, one of the men who led a revolution to bring communism to Russia.

Getting you thinking

What does the word capitalism mean to you? Look up the word in a dictionary to check your definition. Can you give an example of a country that is capitalist?

Communism

Karl Marx and Frederick Engels developed the idea of communism. Marx and Engels were living in England during the Industrial Revolution and this informed their theories.

Marx argued that *capitalism* is a system in which those with money pay those without money to make things for them. They then sell these things for a profit, i.e. for more than they paid the workers to make them. They use this money to hire more people and so on.

Marx argued this system leads to more and more money for only a few people, and that those few people had not created the *product* that they were selling. He thought that eventually the workers – those who made products for a wage – would rise up and overthrow the rich. The system they would set up to replace capitalism would be called communism.

Under communism money would become unimportant; communism would lead to a system where everyone would work for the common good. All property would be owned by everyone, and everyone would decide how society was governed. Marx did not write in much detail about how this system would work in practice, so it was left to others to take his beliefs and try to turn them into a means of running a country. In Russia the man responsible for this was Vladimir Lenin.

Product: an item made for sale

Lenin

Lenin needed to adapt Marx's ideas for many reasons. Russia was not a capitalist country. It had little industry and therefore was not somewhere that Marx would have thought was ready for a communist revolution. The majority of people in Russia were peasant farmers; few could read or write or were involved in politics. Lenin therefore argued that in Russia professional revolutionaries, like himself, would need to educate the *proletariat*. Lenin argued that the revolution might need violence to achieve its ends and that religion and nationalism were ways to keep the poor obedient.

Lenin had fled Russia but as World War One began to go badly and the Tsar was overthrown, he returned to lead his party, the Bolsheviks. In October 1917, he led a second revolution and established the world's first communist state. This was not an easy process and civil war broke out for the next three years. In 1924 Lenin died and his body was *embalmed* and placed on permanent display in Red Square, Moscow where it remains, heavily guarded, today.

Now it's your turn

1 Look at the photograph on the right. What sort of event do you think this is? What does it suggest about the skills political leaders needed to be successful? Are the same skills required by today's politicians?

2 Decide which of the following features are communist and which are capitalist:
   - private property
   - public property
   - private wealth
   - public ownership of wealth
   - classless society
   - society made up of different classes

3 Try to explain why you think each is either communist or capitalist.

Lenin addresses a crowd in Red Square, Moscow, in October 1917

Check your progress

I can talk about some features of communism.
I can describe the difference between communism and capitalism.
I can describe how Lenin is remembered in Russia.

Proletariat: the industrial working class
Embalmed: preserved using chemicals

Reds vs Whites: Civil war in Russia

Objectives

By the end of this lesson you will be able to:

- explain how the Bolsheviks were able to win the civil war
- comment on the methods the Bolsheviks used to get the Russian people on their side

Although Lenin had overthrown the Russian government, he did not defeat all opposition to communist rule. As a result, a civil war broke out in Russia. This section examines how the Bolsheviks won and how they attempted to persuade the Russian people to support them.

Getting you thinking

Russia was an enormous country; what would be some of the problems faced by both armies because of this?

In 1918 Russia divided into two forces: the Reds – made up of the Bolsheviks and led by Trotsky; and the Whites – a force made up of all those who opposed Bolshevik rule. These included the Tsarists, but also the other political parties who had thrown out the Tsar in February only to find themselves thrown out in turn by the Bolsheviks. On the side of the Whites there were also former landowners, former army

A Bolshevik propaganda poster during the Civil War

Nationalised: when factories are taken away from private owners and run by the state The profits then belong to the state

officers and the armies of other powers, such as the French and British. The Whites were led by Generals Yudenich and Denikin and Admiral Kolchak.

Execution of the Tsar

In the summer of 1918, the White Army was approaching Yekaterinburg, where the Tsar and his family were under house arrest. The Bolsheviks decided to execute the Tsar and his entire family.

> As the men began to crowd in through the double doors behind him, Yurovsky (the chief executioner) stood in front of Nicholas … holding a small piece of paper which he began to read: 'In view of the fact that your relatives are continuing their attack on Soviet Russia, the Ural Executive Committee have decided to execute you'. Nicholas turned quickly to look at his family, then turned back to face Yurovsky and said 'What? What?' Yurovsky then repeated what he had said … and shot the Tsar, point blank.
>
> Robert K. Massie, 'The Romanovs: the Final Chapter' (1966)

The aftermath

In 1919, Kolchak was defeated and the foreign armies went home.

The Bolsheviks organised the civilian population with efficiency. They brought in a policy known as War Communism. All factories were *nationalised*. Food was rationed and peasants were forced to give food to the government. Strikes were made illegal and the *Cheka* arrested anyone accused of White support and executed them; over 7,000 people were put to death. The families of important Red Army generals were held hostage to help ensure their continuing loyalty to the Bolsheviks.

A war of ideas

The Bolsheviks made good use of propaganda in the Civil War.

The poster on the left is an example of such propaganda. In the first ten years of Bolshevik rule, over 3,000 different posters like this one were produced to communicate with the Russian people.

One poster asked 'Cossack, who are you with, them or us?' Another showed an image of the peasants being crushed by the rich with the slogan 'The Tsar, the Priest and the Rich Man on the Shoulders of the Labouring People'.

The human cost of the civil war

By November 1920 the White Army was defeated. Over 800,000 soldiers had died, as well as an estimated 8 million civilians, as a result of the famine and disease the war brought with it.

Check your progress

I can give reasons why the Reds won.
I can explain the reasons I have given.
I can identify the most important reason for the Reds' victory.

Now it's your turn

1 What do the actions of the Red Army suggest about how the communists would rule Russia?
2 Why do you think they behaved in this way?

Cheka: the Russian secret police

Fascists and Nazis: Who were they and what did they believe?

After World War One, a new political philosophy developed in Europe; it was called fascism. Italy was the first European country to embrace this philosophy; Mussolini's fascist government came into power in 1922. Fascist beliefs spread to Germany, where they then evolved into Nazism. This section examines Nazism – what it means and what Nazis believed.

Getting you thinking

The poster can tell us a lot about Nazi beliefs. Using the poster, what do you think they thought was important?

What is fascism?

The word 'fascio' is Italian for a group. In 1919 it was used to describe groups that fought against communism in Italy. In 1921 Mussolini founded a National Fascist Party. They had no real beliefs except a hatred of communism and socialism. Over time, however, fascists came to believe that:

- government should be strong
- individuals were not as important as the state
- national pride was important
- expansion of the country was to be encouraged
- the leader was always correct

Baut Jugendherbergen und Heime

Source 1 *Nazi youth hostel poster*

72

In 1921 a party was formed in Germany, the National Socialist Party, or 'Nazis'. By 1923, Adolf Hitler was their leader. The main ideas of Nazism are documented in Hitler's book *Mein Kampf*. The next two sources will help us explore what the Nazis believed.

No more than Nature desires the mating of weaker with stronger individuals, even less does she desire the blending of a higher with a lower race, since, if she did, her whole work of higher breeding, over perhaps hundreds of thousands of years, might be ruined with one blow.

Historical experience offers countless proofs of this. It shows with terrifying clarity that in every mingling of Aryan blood with that of lower peoples the result was the end of the cultured people ... [He] who has remained racially pure and unmixed, has risen to be master of the continent; he will remain the master as long as he does not fall a victim to defilement of the blood.

Source 2 *Adolf Hitler, 'Mein Kampf' (1925)*

German men, German women, German boys, German girls, over a million of you are gathered in many places in all of Germany!

On this the anniversary of the proclamation of the party's programme, you will together swear an oath of loyalty and obedience to Adolf Hitler. You will display to the world what has long been obvious to you, and what you have expressed in past years.

You are swearing your oath on a holiday that Germany celebrates for the first time: Heroes' Memorial Day. We lower our flags in remembrance of those who lived as heroes, and who died as heroes. We lower the flags before the giants of our past, before those who fought for Germany, before the millions who fought in the World War, before those who died preparing the way for the new Reich.

Source 3 *Speech by Rudolph Hess, 25 February 1934 (Rudolph Hess was a leading Nazi)*

Now it's your turn

Use these sources to create a list of Nazi beliefs and explain how you worked these out. For example, if you think the source shows that Nazis believed that cats were the best animals in the world, explain which part of the source material led you to this conclusion.

Check your progress

I can describe what Nazis believed in.
I can use sources to discover what Nazis believed.
I can explain how I reached my conclusions.

Could there have been a British Hitler?

Objectives

By the end of this lesson you will be able to:

- create and support an argument about Hitler's importance as an individual

Sir Oswald Mosley, leader of the British Union of Fascists, pictured receiving the Nazi salute at a Bermondsey rally, 1 May 1938, London, England

Sometimes in history we can try to imagine how the past might have been different. We call this counterfactual history. In this section we are going to think about the differences between Britain and Germany in the 1930s by asking ourselves 'Could there have been a British Hitler?'

Getting you thinking

This is a picture of Oswald Mosley. Mosley was born in 1896. He became the youngest Conservative member of parliament (MP) in 1918. He then became an independent MP before joining the Labour Party in 1926. He was clever and an excellent public speaker and was given a cabinet post in the Labour government of 1929. In 1931 he set up the New Party; but after meeting Mussolini in 1931, he renamed it the British Union of Fascists (BUF).

Proportional representation: a system which allocates seats in parliament based on the percentage of the vote received

How important are individuals? Do they change history or does history make them? Could Mosley have led Germany instead of Hitler if he had been born there?

Let's compare key features of Hitler's life and Mosley's life.

Much was similar about the two men: their political beliefs, their abilities. By 1933, Hitler was chancellor of Germany and had around 43 per cent of the German vote. In 1929 membership of the Nazi party was 129,000. In Germany, MPs were elected using *proportional representation*.

By 1934 the BUF had around 50,000 members. Mosley marched through Jewish parts of London provoking violence and had the support of the Daily Mail. In June 1934, the BUF held a rally in London; when some anti-fascists began heckling him, they were attacked by Mosley's *blackshirts*.

There was an outcry about the violence and the Daily Mail withdrew their support. Mosley, however, continued to campaign; he gave speeches and continued to attract crowds but was unable to gain any election successes. Britain had an election system of *first past the post*.

Hitler	Mosley
Austrian	British
Lower middle class	Upper class
Unsuccessful in early life	Successful career in politics
Good public speaker	Good public speaker
Fought in World War I	Fought in World War I
Leader of political party	Leader of political party
Anti-communist	Anti-communist
Anti-Semitic	Anti-Semitic
Understood the importance of propaganda	Understood the importance of propaganda
Used violence	Used violence

Sir Oswald Mosley provided close on 10,000 people in Olympia tonight with an entertainment which Mr. Bertram Mills might at once have envied and deplored.

For while Mr. Mills must certainly have envied Sir Oswald the number of his audience and the excitement he and his hecklers provided, he must have deplored the violence with which that excitement was obtained...

Inside the great hall it was seen that Sir Oswald Mosley had nothing of theatricalism to learn from either Hitler or Mussolini. There was a massed band of Blackshirts, there were flags, the Union Jack, and the black and yellow flag of the British Union of Fascists.

The Guardian, 8 June 1934

Now it's your turn

Prepare a presentation that answers the question 'would history be different if Hitler was British or Mosley German?'

You will need to consider several factors – the men themselves, the situation in each country – especially the economic situation, and the ways in which political parties were voted for in each country.

Check your progress

I can describe some of the similarities between Hitler and Mosley.

I can decide if history would have been different if Hitler had been British or Mosley had been German, and give reasons.

I can decide the most important factor for determining if history would have been different.

First past the post: a system where each party fights for individual seats and the party with the most seats is given power   Blackshirts: uniformed members of the BUF

What was life like for European Jews between the wars?

In 1933 there were 9.5 million Jewish people living in Europe. They had been part of the continent for hundreds or thousands of years and had contributed enormously to European culture throughout that time. This section examines Jewish life in Europe before World War Two.

Getting you thinking

Jewish wedding procession in Austria, 1934

This picture is of a wedding in Eisenstadt, Austria. What can photographs like this tell us about pre-war Jewish life?

The majority of European Jews lived in the east, in Poland and Russia. Germany had a Jewish population of around half a million and there were around 300,000 Jews living in Britain. In the east, most Jews lived a more traditional life, speaking *Yiddish* and living in small villages, often separated from their neighbours because of *anti-Semitism*. In the west, however, Jews tended to be much more *integrated*. They spoke German, French or English, were educated alongside their fellow citizens and followed lots of different occupations; some were wealthy, some were poor. Many fought in World War One.

Yiddish: spoken language of Jewish people, which originated in Eastern Europe
Anti-Semitism: prejudice against Jewish people

My parents, grandparents and their ancestors came mainly from various parts of the Hapsburg Empire. After World War I, my father went into political exile from Hungary to Vienna where he met my mother. They married and I was born there in 1927. In 1934 … we moved to Gyor in Hungary where my father's family had a contracting and building materials business. Most of the family worked in the firm and my father became their accountant.

Source 1 *John Chillag, 'Survival'*

Life in pre-war Poland was difficult, and even as a child I was acutely aware of anti-Semitism. But my memories of childhood are happy because I grew up in a home where there was love and understanding. I was fortunate to attend an excellent Jewish school, which imbued me with a love of humanity and a strong sense of Jewish identity, security and belonging.

Source 2 *Esther Brunstein, 'Survival'*

My father … transferred his business to Brussels. His financial situation was good and I lived surrounded by luxury. We continued to celebrate the Jewish festivals as we had done in Jerusalem. At school I never felt the need to hide the fact that I was Jewish. Anti-Semitism was never a problem there.

Source 3 *Victoria Ancona Vincent, 'Survival'*

My family is Jewish. My father, the best father in the world, married my mother when he was 36 and she was 25. My sister was born in Frankfurt, in Germany, in 1926. I was born on 12th June 1929. I was four years old when we left Frankfurt. My father emigrated to Holland in 1933 and he is the director of the Dutch Opekta Company. It makes products for making jam.

Source 4 *Anne Frank, 'The Diary of Anne Frank'*

Now it's your turn

1 What does the source material on this page suggest about pre-war Jewish life?
   a) Make a list of information you can find from the sources.
   b) Make a list of information you can *infer* from the sources.
2 Make a list of questions you still have about pre—war life that the source material is not helpful for.
3 How could you go about finding additional source material that could help answer those questions?

Check your progress

I can find out information about Jewish life from the sources.

I can work out what Jewish life was like from the sources.

I can identify areas of missing information from the sources.

Integrated: part of mainstream society
Infer: make guesses based on evidence

What were the Kindertransport?

Objectives

By the end of this lesson you will be able to:

- explain the reasons why the Kindertransport became necessary
- describe the experience of the children involved

Once the Nazis were in power, things began to get very difficult for Germany's Jewish population. Between 1938 and the outbreak of war in 1939, Jewish parents began a movement to save their children. It was called the Kindertransport (Children's Transport). This lesson explores the experience of those children.

Getting you thinking

What does evacuation mean? What kind of people do you think were evacuated in World War Two?

Between 1933 and 1938 the Nazis brought in a series of laws that made life increasingly difficult for Jews. They were banned from marrying non-Jews, from owning businesses, and eventually from going to school. In November 1938, things became much worse with *Kristallnacht* (the Night of Broken Glass); this brought mass organised violence against Jewish property and people (see p. 116). The first Kindertransport left less than a month later in December.

Source 1 Two refugee children arrive in America, New York, 1930s

Kindertransport was similar to evacuation. It was an attempt by parents to send their children somewhere safe and save their lives; sources 2 and 3 are the stories of children who were sent to Britain. Around 10,000 children from Germany, Austria, Poland and Czechoslovakia were sent away on trains and boats by their parents to families in the United Kingdom between December 1938 and May 1940, when the fall of Holland saw the last of the Kindertransport leave.

Many governments across the world refused to accept refugees from Germany, but the British government responded to a campaign and decided to allow children up to the age of 17, who had a bond of £50, to enter the country on a temporary visa. Families of all religions took the children in across Britain.

My next memory is of sitting on Liverpool Street station in London, hearing announcements in a strange language, seeing children all round me being collected and fearing I would be left there alone. At last a lady called Miss Leigh came and took me and two other children in her car... The Christian family who had agreed to take in a refugee child had a daughter who was three years older than me, and who was very kind. Yet I was desperately homesick. Everything was strange: the bread was white, the table manners were different and I could only communicate with signs.

Source 2 *Vera Schaufeld*

We were taken to Butlin's holiday camp in Lowestoft, given two blankets and a wash bowl and shown into a freezing wooden hut with two beds. I was one of about twenty who caught scarlet fever within a week and spent some six weeks in Colchester isolation hospital. I was then taken in by a kindly old lady in her guest house for convalescence. It was here, on my first walk, that a lady came up to me and pressed a shilling into my hand.

Source 3 *Sigi Faith*

Around half of the children lived in schools and hostels; in 1940 around a thousand were interned as enemy aliens by the British government on the Isle of Man. Many of the children who came never saw their family again and settled either in Britain or in Canada and the USA after the war ended.

Now it's your turn

What was life like for the children of the Kindertransport? Can you find positive and negative aspects from the sources?

Check your progress

I can explain why Jewish children left Germany.
I can talk about what they experienced during the Kindertransport.
I can identify both positive and negative experiences that the children had.

Hitler and the rise of Germany

Germany and its neighbours after World War One

The Nazis were nationalists; they believed that Germany was a great country that had been humiliated by the Treaty of Versailles. They aimed to make Germany great again by expanding beyond the borders drawn by Versailles. This section examines how they went about this.

Getting you thinking

When Germany was created in 1870, there were two visions for the country; Kleindeutschland (little Germany), a country that would be made up of the German states, and Grossdeutschland (big Germany), a country that would include all areas in which German was spoken. This included Austria and Alsace. Why do you think Grossdeutschland would have been more attractive to the Nazis?

The Nazis wanted to overturn the Treaty of Versailles and create *Lebensraum* ('living space'). *Lebensraum* would unify all German speakers and meet their needs; oil, rubber, food and slave labour would allow the Reich to grow strong. This, however, required more land.

Rearm: build weapons such as tanks and bombs
Conscription: the process of making all men join the army for a set time

Step 1: Get total control of all German territory and rearm

In 1935 the Saarland voted to reunify with Germany. Hitler announced plans to *rearm* and introduce *conscription* (both of which were forbidden by Versailles). In June 1935, Britain signed an agreement allowing the re-creation of the German navy. In 1936 Hitler took his biggest gamble. The Rhineland was a *demilitarised zone*. Hitler sent troops in. They were outnumbered by the French and they were ordered to withdraw if they faced any opposition; neither France nor Britain reacted. Hitler then began to increase military spending.

Step 2: Create Grossdeutschland

In November 1937 Hitler set out his plans for Austria and Czechoslovakia. In March 1938 the leader of Austria, a Nazi, 'invited' the Germans to occupy Austria to stop a communist plot. The opposition was crushed and 99 out of 100 Austrians voted to become part of Greater Germany. There were 3 million Germans living in Czechoslovakia, a country created by Versailles. The land was rich with minerals and industry; Germany wanted it but Britain was worried. The British prime minister Chamberlain met with Hitler to try to negotiate a compromise. Chamberlain worked to persuade the Czechs to give in to Hitler's demands in return for Hitler being willing to halt all future expansion. The Czechs refused and were excluded from the negotiations. The Germans were given the Sudetenland in western Czechoslovakia and Chamberlain proclaimed that he had created 'peace in our time'.

Step 3: Acquire *Lebensraum*

In March 1939 Hitler took the rest of Czechoslovakia and then turned to Poland. In April, Britain gave Poland a guarantee of help in the case of an attack. In August 1939 Germany and Russia signed a pact agreeing not to fight each other. Then on 1 September Germany invaded Poland. On 3 September, Britain declared war on Germany. World War Two had begun.

Now it's your turn

1. On a map show the area of Germany in 1919, 1936, 1938 and 1939. Use a different colour to show each stage of Hitler's expansion.
2. Why do you think that Britain and France were so unwilling to stop Hitler?
3. Can you identify a 'turning point' when war became inevitable and when Hitler became too strong to stop?

Check your progress

I can describe how Germany grew.

I can give an explanation for why Germany was allowed to grow.

I can identify a date when war became almost certain and explain my answer.

Demilitarised zone: An area where no German soldiers were allowed to be stationed

Communism spreads: China between the wars

Objectives

By the end of this lesson you will be able to:

- assess the importance of Jiang Jieshi and Mao Zedong
- describe the changes taking place in China in the 1920s

Japan fought Germany in World War One. China was supposed to be neutral but parts of it were invaded by the Japanese. The Treaty of Versailles rewarded Japan with some Chinese territory. This caused a great deal of unrest in China. This section examines how China and Japan developed in the 1920s and 1930s.

Getting you thinking

In 1920 China was corrupt and dangerous. There was no clear leadership; parts of the country were ruled by warlords, while other parts were ruled by foreign powers such as the Japanese. The people of China were very unhappy about this. How could ordinary people change the way their country was run? Suggest at least three ways they might have done this.

A patriotic demonstration during the Chinese-Japanese War, 1937–1941

Changing China

Two men emerged as important figures: Jiang Jieshi (Chiang Kai-Shek) and Mao Zedong. Jiang was from a rich family. He belonged to the Guomindung (GMD) a party with three principles: nationalism, democracy and social reform. Mao was from a prosperous family, though his father had been born a peasant; he became a communist. The GMD was not a communist party but in 1923 it allowed communists to join and accepted help from Russia. In 1925 Jiang became leader of the GMD and immediately began to expel the communists. Mao and the communists fled to northwest China. In 1927 the GMD massacred 5,000 communists in Shanghai and Jiang continued to hate them more than the Japanese.

By 1928 the GMD had captured Beijing and ruled much of China. Jiang did reform the education system and improve the roads. However, he ignored most of the three principles. There were no elections, foreigners were not driven out and the rights of the peasants were ignored.

The communists fled to Hunan province in the north; Mao decided to change the principles of the communist party and said that peasants, not town workers, would lead the revolution. Jiang attempted to wipe them out, but Mao had four principles for fighting:

- If the enemy attacks, retreat.
- When the enemy camps, harass.
- If the enemy tires, attack.
- When the enemy retreats, pursue.

By 1931 the GMD had lost 23,000 men, but Mao was still alive.

In 1931 Japan took more Chinese territory by invading Manchuria. Jiang continued to attack Mao rather than the Japanese. He attempted to encircle the communists. Mao decided to escape; 120,000 communist men, women and children marched 6,000 miles to escape further north. Only 20,000 survived, including Mao who began to re-establish the party.

Jiang continued to rule as he had before. Between 1929 and 1933, 6 million peasants died of starvation and by 1936 the Japanese had gained control of five provinces. Jiang sent his general to wipe out Mao; instead he signed a truce with him and they agreed to fight the Japanese together. Jiang tried to stop this but was arrested by his own men. He agreed to stop fighting the communists and work to fight the Japanese. In 1937 the Chinese-Japanese War began.

Now it's your turn

1 Draw a graph comparing the fortunes of Jiang and Mao between 1920 and 1937. The vertical axis represents success and failure. The horizontal axis shows the years.
2 Overall, who was the more successful of the two men?
3 How did things stay the same in China between 1920 and 1937? How did they change?

Check your progress

I can complete a graph showing the high and low points of Jiang and Mao's career.

I can say who was the most successful man and explain why.

I can identify continuities and changes in China.

How did war affect the Chinese people?

Objectives

By the end of this lesson you will be able to:

- give examples of the consequences of the Chinese-Japanese war
- use evidence to support your conclusions

Japan was ruled by an emperor, Hirohito. The Japanese believed that their emperor was a god. Japan's victory in World War One and its defeat of Russia in 1905 had made it a powerful force in Asia. This lesson examines the Chinese-Japanese war between 1937 and 1941.

Getting you thinking

In 1927 Japanese prime minister Baron Tanaka wrote a statement outlining Japan's aims. He wanted to conquer eastern Asia, defeat the USA and seize Manchuria and Mongolia. In 1931 at least one of these aims was achieved with the invasion of Manchuria – but Japan wanted more. On 28 July 1937 Tanaka launched a full-scale war by air and land. By August Japan was attacking Shanghai; Jiang's forces held out for three months but the city fell in December. That same month the Japanese began the invasion of Nanking.

Through wholesale atrocities and vandalism at Nanking, the Japanese Army has thrown away a rare opportunity to gain the respect and confidence of the Chinese inhabitants and of foreign opinion there.

The killing of civilians was widespread. Foreigners who travelled widely through the city Wednesday found civilian dead on every street. Some of the victims were aged men, women and children.

Policemen and firemen were special objects of attack. Many victims were bayoneted and some of the wounds were barbarously cruel.

Any person who ran because of fear or excitement was likely to be killed on the spot as was any one caught by roving patrols in streets or alleys after dark. Many slayings were witnessed by foreigners.

The Japanese looting amounted almost to plundering of the entire city. Nearly every building was entered by Japanese soldiers, often under the eyes of their officers, and the men took whatever they wanted. The Japanese soldiers often impressed Chinese to carry their loot.

The mass executions of war prisoners added to the horrors the Japanese brought to Nanking. After killing the Chinese soldiers who threw down their arms and surrendered, the Japanese combed the city for men in civilian garb who were suspected of being former soldiers.

In one building in the refugee zone 400 men were seized. They were marched off, tied in batches of fifty, between lines of riflemen and machine gunners, to the execution ground.'

Source 1 *'Aboard the U.S.S. Oahu at Shanghai',*
The New York Times, 17 December 1937

Atrocities: acts of exceptional brutality and violence
Vandalism: wilful destruction of property

Source 2 *Prideaux-Brune, the British Consul, telegram, 11 January 1938.*

TELEGRAM

SITUATION HERE IS FAR MORE ABNORMAL THAN WE HAD ANTICIPATED. ATROCITIES COMMITTED HERE IN THE FIRST TWO WEEKS AFTER THE OCCUPATION OF THE CITY WERE OF A NATURE AND ON A SCALE WHICH ARE ALMOST INCREDIBLE. CONDITIONS WITH REGARDS TO MILITARY UNRULINESS ARE SLOWLY IMPROVING BUT ISOLATED CASES OF MURDER AND OTHER BARBARITIES CONTINUE.

Jiang and the communists retreated and used guerrilla tactics to fight the Japanese until the bombing of Pearl Harbour in 1941.

Now it's your turn

1 Looking at the sources, what were the consequences of the Japanese invasion?
2 What questions do you still have that the source material is unable to answer?

Check your progress

★ I can describe the consequences of the Japanese invasion.
★★ I can use source material to support my account.
★★★ I can recognise the limitations of the source material.

Jiang Jieshi, the Chinese president, in 1931

Barbarously: very cruelly
Plundering: wholesale theft of valuables

How did the world try to prevent war?

Objectives

By the end of this lesson you will be able to:

- identify the strengths and weaknesses of the League of Nations
- make a judgement about the League's overall success

After the end of World War One, the powers at Versailles decided to establish an organisation designed to prevent war breaking out again. It was named the League of Nations. This section examines the league and explores its effectiveness.

Getting you thinking

What organisations do we have today that are designed to stop conflict? Do they work?

The League of Nations was an attempt to stop war. It had 26 articles that aimed to reduce arms and to stop war, either through *sanctions* or military action. The League also established a Court of International Justice at The Hague to allow nations to bring their disputes before a court. It had limited powers and could not force a country to accept its judgement.

The League's first meeting was in 1922 and 42 nations attended. However, some important countries were missing: neither Russia nor any of the defeated powers were allowed to join, while the USA refused to join.

Despite this the League had some successes. For example, it organised financial help for Austria in 1922 when the country was on the verge of economic collapse. In 1925 the League stopped Greece from invading Bulgaria and by 1939, it had settled 70 cases and arranged 400 agreements. These, however, were minor disputes. The first real test for the League came with Japan's invasion of Manchuria in 1931.

Manchuria

Japan was a member of the League of Nations. The League sent a commission whose report condemned the invasion. When the League refused to accept the occupation of Manchuria, the Japanese ignored it and left the group in 1933.

Abyssinia

Italy was a member of the League, as was Abyssinia (now Ethiopia). Mussolini wanted to expand Italy's territory abroad. In 1935, Italy began to amass troops on the Abyssinian borders and Abyssinia

Sanctions: peaceful actions against a country aimed at forcing it to change

THE MAN WHO TOOK THE LID OFF.

Source 1 *A Daily Mail cartoon of the Italian dictator, Benito Mussolini*

appealed to the League for help. Italy invaded using planes and poison gas to defeat the Abyssinians. Although the League applied economic sanctions against Italy, it excluded coal, steel and oil from the list. The Italians traded with Germany, Austria and the USA, while Britain and France continued to allow Italy to use the Suez Canal. In 1937 Italy left the League.

Source 2 *Statement about a meeting between British prime minister Stanley Baldwin and a deputation from the League of Nations on 13 December 1935*

The Prime Minster said that the League policy is still the policy of the Government and we were all in agreement in desiring that the policy should be effective... He then explained the great gravity of the European situation, including the danger that Mussolini might make a 'mad dog' attack on the British fleet. Though the result of such an attack must in the long run be the defeat of Italy, the war might last some time and produce both losses and diplomatic complications of a serious kind. Meantime we were bound to consider whether we could rely on effective support from any other member of the League. No member except Great Britain has made any preparations for meeting an attack.

Now it's your turn

1 Look at Source 1. Who is in the cartoon? What does the title of the cartoon mean? Do you think the cartoonist likes the League?
2 Was the League of Nations a success or failure? Examine the evidence for both arguments and make a judgement.

Check your progress

I can make a judgement about the League of Nations.
I can identify the League's strengths and weaknesses.
I can explain my judgement using evidence.

The Spanish Civil War

Objectives

By the end of this lesson you will be able to:

- identify the causes of the Spanish Civil War
- identify the ways in which the war has been represented

The world was an unsettled place in the 1930s. In this lesson we will examine the war that broke out in Europe before World War Two – the Spanish Civil War.

Getting you thinking

This is Picasso's painting of Guernica, a town which was bombed in the Spanish Civil War. Can you find in the picture:

- people dying?
- a woman weeping over a dead child?
- a horse dying from a wound in its side?

In 1931 the Spanish king *abdicated* as conflict between the rich and the poor grew. Elections were held and a *coalition government* was set up. Women were given the right to vote. Land reform was attempted; tenant farmers were given the right to buy their land, but the landowners had to be *compensated* and the government did not have the money to do this. The church was one of the biggest landowners and many peasants attacked it as a symbol of the unfairness in Spain.

In 1933 a fascist party was set up in Spain called the Falange; they became known as the Nationalists. Between 1933 and 1936, different parties from the left and right ruled. In 1936 violence broke out, especially against the church. Peasants seized land from landowners.

Abdicated: stood down
Coalition government: a government made up of different parties who have agreed to cooper

The Nationalists led by Franco, a Spanish general, rebelled. The Republican government organised their own troops and civil war broke out.

Germany and Italy helped the Nationalists; the Russians supported the Republicans. Many people went to Spain to fight for the Republicans in the International Brigade.

The American author Ernest Hemingway fought for the Republicans, and after the war he wrote a novel. The extract on the right describes an American meeting with other soldiers to plan a mission to blow up train lines carrying supplies for the fascists.

Laurie Lee was an Englishman who volunteered for the Republican cause. He wrote '*A Moment of War*' (1991). The extract below describes soldiers looking for fascists during bombing attacks.

> 'I have heard much good of you.' said Robert Jordan.
> 'What have you heard of me?' asked Pablo.
> 'I have heard that you are an excellent guerrilla leader, that you are loyal to the Republic and prove your loyalty through your acts. I bring you greetings from the general staff.'
>
> Ernest Hemingway, 'For whom the bell tolls' (1940)

> It had happened before, when night-shelling was heavy and precise – someone, some 'Franco agent', would have been flashing a torch from a rooftop, and then, when the bombardment was heaviest, would toss a few grenades down into the street to confuse the fire-trucks and rescue parties.
> After two winters of siege, the inside war was still active, and not everyone, even in this poor bare tavern … could be absolutely sure of the man who sat beside him.
> 'We caught one of them, anyway,' the younger soldier said fiercely. 'Running across the tiles with a cart lamp.'
> 'Could have been trying to save his skin,' said someone.
> 'Did you arrest him?'
> 'Hell, no. We just threw him off the roof. He'd done enough. His body's outside in a barrow.'
>
> Laurie Lee, 'A Moment of War' (1991)

Now it's your turn APP

1 All three sources were created by Republican supporters. What images of the war do they each portray?
2 Are they the same?
3 They are all from one side of the conflict. Does this mean that they are of no use to historians?

Check your progress

I can get information about the war from the sources.

I can identify the ways in which the sources agree or disagree.

I can recognise the strengths and limitations of the sources.

Compensated: *given money to make up for their loss*

Name that period!

This unit has examined the 1920s and the 1930s. For most people this period is known as the inter-war period. In this final section you are going to consider the main features of the time and decide on a more appropriate name.

Getting you thinking

Historians often name periods. For example, the Renaissance implies that the key feature of that time was a rebirth of knowledge. The Enlightenment implies a time in which human understanding made great progress. This period is named most often by the two events that signal its beginning and end, World War One and World War Two. This implies that the 1920s and 1930s themselves are less important than what happened before and after them. Do you think this is true?

You need to review the evidence for the time and complete the following activities.

The age of money

What evidence is there that this period can be called the age of money? This would imply that the economic growth and subsequent Depression were the most significant features of the period. Find evidence to support this view.

The age of political extremes

What evidence is there that this period can be called the age of political extremes? This would imply that it is politics rather than money that is the most significant feature of the age. Find evidence to support this view.

Hammer and sickle

Swastika

The age of racism

What evidence is there that this period can be called the age of racism? This would imply that it is racial hatred rather than money or politics that defines the period. Find evidence to support this view.

Ku Klux Klansman (left), Kristallnacht – the 'Night of Broken Glass' (right))

Assessment task

1 Which of the names do you feel best represents the 1920s and 1930s? You can choose one of the above or develop your own name with evidence to support your choice.

2 Having chosen your own name for the period, create a front cover for a history book of that title. Your cover needs to have images that illustrate your choice of title and a summary on the back of at least 200 words to explain the book's contents.

This work sums up all you have understood about the period and you need to use your skills of description and communication. You will also need to think about the concepts of historical significance (*what* makes something important?), and historical interpretation (*how* should the past be remembered?).

Check your level

I can describe the key characteristics of the 1920s and 1930s, and can decide a name for the period.	I can describe the key characteristics of the 1920s and 1930s. I can decide on a name for the period and justify my choice of name.	I understand that it is tricky to apply just one label to a period, because different things might be important in different parts of the world and at different times in the 1920s and 1930s.
Level 5	Level 6	Level 7

Objectives

By the end of this unit you will be able to:

- explain some of the causes of World War Two
- discuss the role of some significant individuals during the war
- explore how the nature of war changed from WW1 to WW2

Churchill's speech

Speaking to the House of Commons the day after being made prime minister, Churchill said:

I have nothing to offer but blood, toil, tears, and sweat. We have before us an ordeal of the most grievous kind. We have before us many, many months of struggle and suffering.

You ask, what is our policy? I say it is to wage war by land, sea, and air. War with all our might and with all the strength God has given us, and to wage war against a monstrous tyranny never surpassed in the dark and *lamentable* catalogue of human crime. That is our policy.

You ask, what is our aim? I can answer in one word. It is victory. Victory at all costs – victory in spite of all terrors – victory, however long and hard the road may be, for without victory there is no survival.'

Lamentable: unfortunate, sad

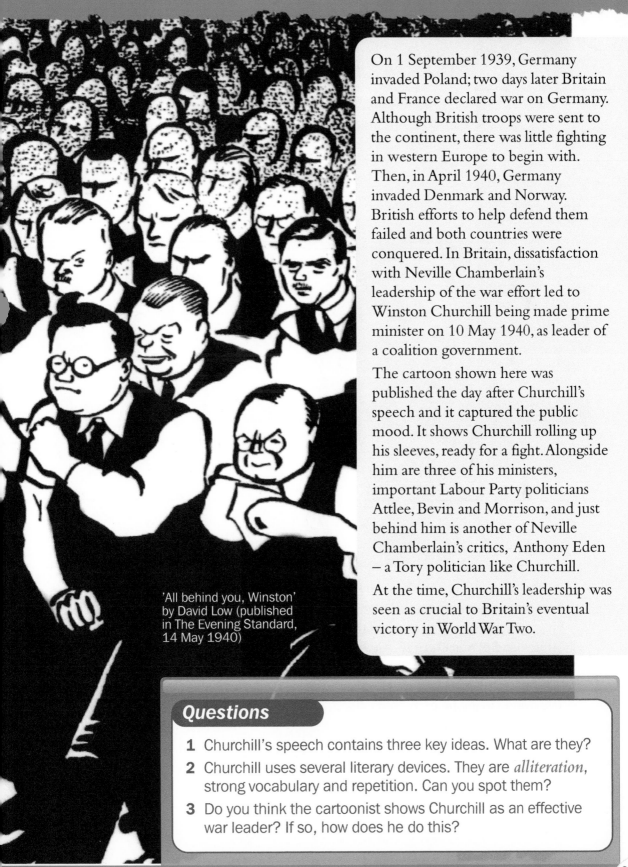

On 1 September 1939, Germany invaded Poland; two days later Britain and France declared war on Germany. Although British troops were sent to the continent, there was little fighting in western Europe to begin with. Then, in April 1940, Germany invaded Denmark and Norway. British efforts to help defend them failed and both countries were conquered. In Britain, dissatisfaction with Neville Chamberlain's leadership of the war effort led to Winston Churchill being made prime minister on 10 May 1940, as leader of a coalition government.

The cartoon shown here was published the day after Churchill's speech and it captured the public mood. It shows Churchill rolling up his sleeves, ready for a fight. Alongside him are three of his ministers, important Labour Party politicians Attlee, Bevin and Morrison, and just behind him is another of Neville Chamberlain's critics, Anthony Eden – a Tory politician like Churchill.

At the time, Churchill's leadership was seen as crucial to Britain's eventual victory in World War Two.

'All behind you, Winston' by David Low (published in The Evening Standard, 14 May 1940)

Questions

1 Churchill's speech contains three key ideas. What are they?

2 Churchill uses several literary devices. They are *alliteration*, strong vocabulary and repetition. Can you spot them?

3 Do you think the cartoonist shows Churchill as an effective war leader? If so, how does he do this?

Alliteration: repetition of the same consonant sound at the start of two or more words that are near each other

Did Germany cause World War Two?
Part 1

Objectives

By the end of this lesson you will be able to:

- describe the steps leading to World War Two
- decide whether Hitler was to blame for starting the war

During World War One people felt they were fighting the war to end all wars, but just twenty years later, a second and more devastating war had begun. Why did this happen?

Well I think that Hitler and his aggressive policies caused the war. First he marched his troops into the Rhineland in March 1936. Next he marched into Austria in March 1938, into Czechoslovakia in September 1938 and finally he attacked Poland. In his book *Mein Kampf* he said he was going to conquer land to the east and create a greater Germany, and that is exactly what he did when he came to power. So he was to blame.

I'm sorry but I can't entirely agree with you. Hitler might have been leader of Germany but he was just one man. The idea of a 'greater Germany' had the majority of the German people and German history behind it. So if you are going to blame anyone, then it is the people of Germany standing behind Hitler.

Yes and you have to consider the importance of the Treaty of Versailles. That was an unfair settlement. Germany had to accept the blame for World War One and lost territory in Europe as well as her empire. And there were the *reparations*. Demanding such a huge amount of money, £6.6 billion, from Germany was bad enough, but the continuing arguments about payment kept the German people resentful for years afterwards. No wonder people supported Hitler when he said he would restore Germany's greatness. It was the men who agreed the Treaty of Versailles who were really responsible for the war.

Well, I think you are all forgetting that it was Britain and France that declared war on Germany, not the other way round. They were prepared to fight a war because they wanted to protect their position as great powers in Europe and the world. And that is the other issue we should consider. It was not just a European war but a world war, and Britain and France wanted to protect their empires in Africa, the Middle East and Asia.

Now it's your turn

1 Make a timeline of the events leading up to the outbreak of World War Two. Read the discussion of these four historians to find this information.
2 Now think about their arguments. Each of them has a different explanation for why World War Two began. They agree on what the causes were but seem to disagree about which was most important. Your task is to explore what happened and then to decide if Hitler was to blame for starting the war.

Check your progress

   I can describe some of the main events leading up to the start of World War Two.
   I can identify some causes of World War Two.
   I can can explain who I think was responsible, and give reasons.

Reparations: payments by Germany for the damaged caused in World War One

PEACE AND FUTURE CANNON FODDER

The Tiger: "Curious! I seem to hear a child weeping!"

'Peace and future cannon fodder', a cartoon by Will Dyson, published in the *Daily Herald*, May 1919

Britain and France went to war to protect Poland; they declared war on Germany after Hitler invaded it.

That is true, but then why did Britain and France do nothing to protect Czechoslovakia in 1938? And it is worth pointing out that in the war roughly 280,000 Czechs died but 6.8 million Poles died. So who was helped the most?

You have to think about what sort of war Hitler and Germany wanted, too. The attack on Poland was intended as a *blitzkrieg*, a swift victory. The Germans never intended to start a total war.

Yes I think you are right about that. And another point to support that claim is that the Germans agreed to split Poland with the USSR. People tend to forget that the USSR also invaded Poland a fortnight after the Germans did in 1939. Hitler was surprised that the British and French decided to support Poland. But I'd like to go back to Versailles. That treaty tried to preserve the position of Britain and France as great powers and ignored the development of Italy, Japan, and the USSR as great powers too. So it was inevitable that these countries would try to build new empires of their own.

Certainly Germany, Italy and Japan were all aggressive in the 1930s. Italy tried to build its empire by attacking Abyssinia in October 1935 and Albania in April 1939; Japan attacked China in July 1937 (see page 84). And all three countries were in one alliance.

Blitzkrieg: literally 'lightning war', quick surprise strikes with support from warplanes

I agree that Britain and France were worried by Japan's aggression, which threatened their colonies in Asia, and by Italy's aggression, which threatened their colonies in Africa. In fact, I think they were more concerned about that than Hitler's actions in Europe.

The two other great powers, the USA and the USSR, were also worried but took no action. The USSR was weakened by internal conflict and Stalin's purges; the USA had retreated into isolationism, a policy of not getting involved in world affairs – although they did try to limit the power of Japan with trade restrictions. That is part of the reason why the League of Nations was unable to keep the peace in the 1930s; because the great powers were either not in it, not prepared to act, or were the problem themselves.

So you think it all comes down to the great powers competing for power and empire?

I do, and I think that helps to explain why Hitler invaded the USSR in June 1941, because he knew that Germany and the USSR would have to fight for control of Eastern Europe eventually. It is also why the Japanese attacked the USA at Pearl Harbour in December 1941. They knew they would have to fight for control of the Pacific region.

That certainly is the moment when the separate wars in Europe and Asia came together into a single global conflict. So are we blaming everyone?

Well, I still think that without Hitler there would have been no war.

And I would still go back to the Treaty of Versailles.

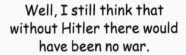

Check your progress

⭐ I can describe some of the main events leading up to the start of World War Two and place them in a chronological framework.

⭐⭐ I can identify some causes of the war.

⭐⭐⭐ I can explain who was responsible for the war, and give reasons.

Extension work

If this discussion had been part of a documentary on television, there might have been a presenter who summarised the arguments and offered a conclusion. Can you write that brief summary and conclusion?

Was World War Two a global war?

The map is a view of the world in 1939-1945, showing the countries that fought on the side of the Allies (led by Britain, France, Russia and later the United States) and on the side of the Axis (led by Germany). The dates in brackets show when they joined the war. European countries that remained neutral are white on the map. Some of the major land and sea battles of World War Two are also marked, with the dates when they happened.

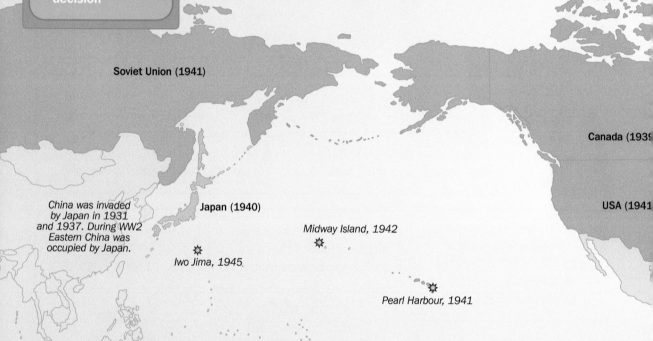

Soviet Union (1941)

Canada (1939

China was invaded by Japan in 1931 and 1937. During WW2 Eastern China was occupied by Japan.

Japan (1940)

USA (1941

Midway Island, 1942

Iwo Jima, 1945

Pearl Harbour, 1941

Australia (1939)

New Zealand (1939)

The main Allied and Axis powers in World War Two, and some of the key battles

Now it's your turn

Using the information on the map, decide whether World War Two was a global war. There are a number of criteria you might use to help you to decide:

- number of countries involved
- number of countries not involved
- number of countries in which land fighting took place
- the range of continents on which fighting happened, and how far these are apart
- areas of sea on which fighting took place

Check your progress

I can investigate an historical problem.
I can use a range of evidence to make a judgement.
I can decide whether World War Two was a global war, and give reasons.

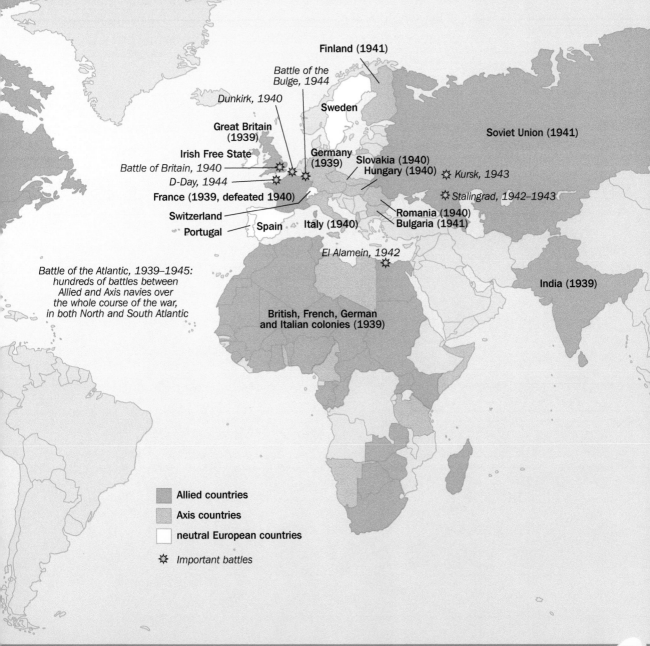

Finland (1941)

Battle of the Bulge, 1944

Dunkirk, 1940

Sweden

Great Britain (1939)

Soviet Union (1941)

Irish Free State

Battle of Britain, 1940

D-Day, 1944

France (1939, defeated 1940)

Germany (1939)

Slovakia (1940)
Hungary (1940)

☼ Kursk, 1943

☼ Stalingrad, 1942–1943

Switzerland

Portugal

Spain

Italy (1940)

Romania (1940)
Bulgaria (1941)

Battle of the Atlantic, 1939–1945: hundreds of battles between Allied and Axis navies over the whole course of the war, in both North and South Atlantic

El Alamein, 1942 ☼

India (1939)

British, French, German and Italian colonies (1939)

Allied countries

Axis countries

neutral European countries

☼ Important battles

Evacuation

As war approached, children under the age of 11 and mothers with children under five were evacuated from cities. They were taken to areas where they would be safe from the bombing, which was expected to kill thousands of people.

Getting you thinking

Try to imagine what it must have felt like to be told you were leaving home and going to live with strangers. Think about what you could take with you – one small suitcase of possessions and your gas mask. What would you pack and what would you leave behind? Imagine saying goodbye to your family and travelling with your school friends and teachers to a new home. What would it be like living in the country? Imagine all those new sights and sounds! This is what happened to thousands of children in September 1939.

Objectives

By the end of this lesson you will be able to:

- explore what it was like for children to be evacuated during World War Two

Child evacuees at a railway station in London in September 1939

Read the evidence below which describes what some people remember of evacuation.

Mrs Dransfield was extremely strict. She had no children of her own and her home was her palace and I was a bit of an intruder.

...I felt very homesick and I longed for letters from my mother and I used to kiss her photograph 'goodnight' every night...

I got my love of the country from this time. We had plenty of eggs, butter and milk as I used to go round the farms to collect these. I was sent to the little village school and I loved it.

Angela Sexton

The foster mum thought she was on to a good thing with me and the other eleven-year-old girl billeted with her. I think she regarded it as a business transaction. We were expected to shop and wash up and look after a whining three-year-old. I got my own back by teaching the three year old some fruity London street terms. This was one way of repaying her for all the drudgery she was subjecting me to.

Mary Baxter, interviewed in 1988

Evacuation was the most exciting thing that happened to me. After school we were expected to work, sweeping out Mr Benson's butcher's shop and scrubbing down the marble slabs and great wooden chopping blocks ... Once a week we were bathed in the kitchen where Mrs Benson would have the tin bath ready in front of the fire, full of hot water. We were never hungry ... I played in the fields and moors with the village boys, bird nesting and trying to snare rabbits. Once we spent an afternoon damming up a stream. In the night it flooded the church and six houses. The vicar caned us all. I had never been caned before, but we deserved it...

A former evacuee remembers his experiences as a 13-year-old boy

Now it's your turn APP

1 Complete the table below:

Good things about evacuation	Bad things about evacuation

2 Why do you think experiences of evacuation varied so much? Explain your answer.
3 All of the evidence above was written by people many years after they had been evacuated. Does this affect the usefulness and reliability of the evidence? Explain your answer.
4 Do you think it was cruel to separate children from their families? Why do you think this?

Check your progress

I can describe what it was like to be evacuated.
I can see that people had good experiences and bad experiences.
I can understand why evacuation experiences varied so much.

Billeted: *made to live with*
Drudgery: *boring, repetitive housework and jobs*

Which were the most important turning points of the war?
Part 1

Objectives

By the end of this lesson you will be able to:

- explain what a turning point is
- begin to recognise and explain why some events might be judged as more historically significant than others

In his play 'The History Boys' Alan Bennett describes turning points as 'moments when history rattles over the points'. By this Bennett means when events take a new direction.

Getting you thinking

Your task is to decide which, if any, of the four following events can be described as a turning point for World War Two. To help you decide, complete the following table for each event:

Event		
Event description		
Short-term consequences		
Long-term consequences		
Turning point	Yes	No

Enigma

In the summer of 1939 a team of scholars arrived at Bletchley Park in Buckinghamshire. They had been recruited because they were chess champions, crossword experts or mathematicians. Their mission was to crack the Nazis' Enigma code.

Dougray Scott and Kate Winslet in a scene from the film *Enigma*

The Germans were convinced that Enigma could not be broken and so they used the *Enigma machine* for all military and intelligence communications. This meant that if the British and their allies could break Enigma and decode these messages, they would learn what the Germans were planning. This would give them an important advantage. By 1945, over 9,000 people were working at Bletchley Park.

Enigma machine: a machine used to encode and decode secret messages

The code-breakers were given a good start by Polish mathematicians who had been working on breaking Enigma for several years, and who had even built replicas of the Enigma machine. These were given to the British before Poland was conquered. Enigma was cracked in 1940, although the code did not stay broken. The Germans made continual changes to improve it and so the code-breaking work continued throughout the war.

The intelligence that was learned was code-named ULTRA. It was only made available to a few commanders in order to prevent the Germans from realising that it had been broken. Two areas of war in which it made a great difference were in ensuring that Rommel did not capture Egypt in 1942 and that Britain won the Battle of the Atlantic. Historians cannot agree on its overall importance. Some argue it shortened the war by as much as two years. After the war, Churchill referred to the Bletchley staff as: 'My geese that laid the golden eggs and never cackled'.

Pearl Harbour

On the morning of Sunday 7 December 1940, the Japanese launched a surprise attack on the US naval base at Pearl Harbour in Hawaii from six aircraft carriers. It was a military success. Of the eight battleships of the US Pacific Fleet, two were destroyed, three severely damaged and three damaged. Three light cruisers were also damaged. Of the 394 aircraft on the island, 164 were destroyed and 159 damaged. In addition, 2,395 service personnel and civilians were killed, and 1,178 wounded. The Japanese lost just 29 aircraft and five midget submarines; only 65 of their men were killed or wounded.

The US battleships California and Oklahoma are hit, during the Japanese attack on Pearl Harbour

However, the three aircraft carriers of the Pacific Fleet were at sea and so were undamaged. Moreover the dockyard and fuel supplies were not damaged, so the Pacific Fleet still had its most important ships and an operating base. Immediately after what they saw as their military triumph, the Japanese began their conquest of the Philippines from the USA, of Malaya, Burma and Hong Kong from Britain, and the East Indies from Holland, in addition to their conquests in China and French Indochina.

However, the attack also brought the USA into the war and it could be argued that with its huge industrial resources and population, defeat for Japan was inevitable. Four days after the Pearl Harbour attacks, Germany and Italy declared war on the USA.

Which were the most important turning points of the war?
Part 2

Soviet troops attacking in the Battle of Kursk, 1943

Kursk

On 5 July 1943 the Germans launched a new *blitzkrieg* offensive on the eastern front, at Kursk in Russia. However, it was not a surprise; delays in equipment meant that the Germans had postponed the attack several times. The Soviets, who were expecting it, had made massive preparations. So when the attack began, the Soviet army was ready.

The Germans attacked with 900,000 soldiers, 10,000 artillery guns, 2,700 tanks and 2,000 aircraft. This was roughly one third of Germany's total military strength. Opposing them the Russians had 1,300,000 soldiers, 20,000 artillery guns, 3,600 tanks and 2,400 aircraft.

By 12 July the attack had ground to a halt, with massive German losses in men (500,000 killed, wounded or missing) and equipment. For the first time a blitzkrieg had been stopped. The Soviet army then launched its own offensives and pushed the Germans back more than 60 miles in some places.

The Germans were never able to attack on the eastern front again – from Kursk onwards they were always on the defensive; the initiative lay with the Soviet armies.

Although often thought of as a tank battle, Kursk as a whole arguably demonstrated the triumph of artillery, infantry and engineers over armour. The Soviet plan was to soak up the German assault in a colossal web of defensive positions, and only then launch their armoured counter-attack. It was also an important air battle, in which the balance now shifted in the favour of the Soviets.

John Keegan, Atlas of World War II (2006)

D-Day

On 6 June 1944 American, British, Canadian and Free French forces landed on five beaches along a 50-mile stretch of the Normandy coastline. Code-named Operation Overlord, this was the largest *amphibious* invasion ever mounted. It involved 175,000 allied soldiers, sailors and airmen and approximately 7,000 ships and 11,500 aircraft. There had been a range of diversionary activities, so the Germans were not expecting the landings at this point or at this time – surprise was achieved. However, the fighting on the beaches was fierce. The Allies had over ten thousand casualties, 4,500 of whom died – mostly airborne troops or those who had landed at Omaha Beach. The Germans lost between 4,000 and 9,000 men.

By the end of the day, the Allied forces had successfully established a beach-head from which they were later able to break out. The battle for Normandy that followed lasted until mid-August. By the time it had finished the German armies were in retreat. In addition to military casualties, 15–20,000 French civilians were killed, mostly through Allied bombing.

D-Day marked the start of a second front. From that day onwards the German armies had to fight a war on two fronts, something they had always tried to avoid. The Allied armies were eventually able to liberate France, Belgium and the Netherlands and advance into Germany itself.

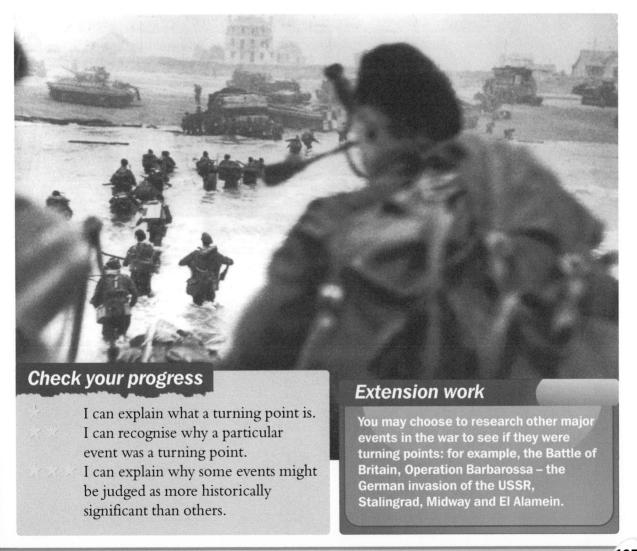

Allied troops landing on the Normandy beaches on D-Day, 6 June 1944

Check your progress

I can explain what a turning point is.
I can recognise why a particular event was a turning point.
I can explain why some events might be judged as more historically significant than others.

Extension work

You may choose to research other major events in the war to see if they were turning points: for example, the Battle of Britain, Operation Barbarossa – the German invasion of the USSR, Stalingrad, Midway and El Alamein.

Amphibious: involving attack on both sea and land

World War Two: the stories of individuals

Objectives

By the end of this lesson you will be able to:

- recount some of the individual stories of World War Two
- begin to recognise the diversity of experiences of war across the globe in April 1943

Josef Stalin, leader of the USSR, said, 'A single death is a tragedy; a million deaths is a statistic.' So far we have taken the big view of World War Two and looked at global events and turning points, and we have looked at casualties as statistics. But what about the individual human stories behind them? That is an approach that the historian Martin Gilbert takes. He goes through the war on a daily basis, focusing not on the big but on the small events.

Getting you thinking

Second World War was first published in 1989. Its author, the historian Martin Gilbert, begins it like this: '…the Second World War was among the most destructive conflicts in human history; more than forty-six million soldiers and civilians died, many in circumstances of prolonged and horrifying cruelty.'

You are going to explore one month of the war, April 1943. While Gilbert describes the deaths as a 'tragedy', he speaks also of 'the courage of soldiers, sailors and airmen, the courage of partisans and resistance fighters, and the courage of those who, starving, naked and without strength or weapons, were sent to their deaths.'

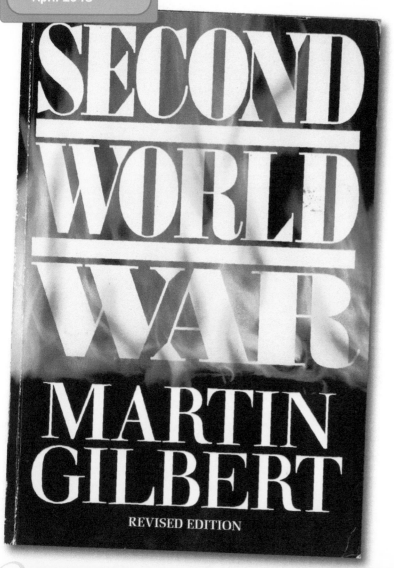

Cover of Martin Gilbert's book *Second World War*

4 April, 1943

The eight crew of the Liberator bomber Lady Be Good took part in the bombing of the docks at Naples. 221 Italians were killed. On their way back to base the crew got lost over the Libyan desert, ran out of fuel and baled out and then tried to walk out of the desert.

5 April

Dietrich Bonhoeffer, a Protestant pastor who spoke out against Nazism, was arrested in Berlin and charged with 'subverting the armed forces'. He was imprisoned and eventually executed in Flossenburg concentration camp in April 1945.

16 April

French resistance member Olivier Giran was executed.

18 April

Four days earlier the US Navy had decoded a message giving the detailed movements of Admiral Yamamoto, head of the Japanese navy and planner of Pearl Harbour. His plane was ambushed by US fighters over Bougainville Island and shot down. He died.

19 April

When the Germans tried to restart the deportations of Jews from the Warsaw Ghetto they were met with resistance. Although poorly armed, with a few rifles and home-made grenades, the Jewish fighters managed to resist for three weeks. In the fighting 300 Germans and 7,000 Jews died.

In Tunisia, Maori Private Tepene Heka killed several Italian soldiers and captured an anti-tank gun, three machine guns and fourteen Italians single-handed. He was awarded the Distinguished Conduct Medal.

20 April

It was announced in Washington that a number of American airmen shot down over Tokyo had been beheaded.

23 April

Kapitänleutnant Helmut Fiehn and his crew of 55 men died when their submarine, U191, was depth-charged by HMS Hesperus southeast of Iceland.

29 April

Six British commandos were captured after placing limpet mines on German ships in Haugesund Fjord. They were sent to Sachsenhausen concentration camp. One commando called Mayer, suspected of being Jewish, was taken away and was never heard of again.

Now it's your turn

1 Are tragedy and courage the most appropriate words to describe the war?
2 Which other words would you add?

Check your progress

I can recount some of the individual stories of World War Two.
I can begin to recognise the diversity of experience.
I can reach a judgement about whether to see the loss of a life as a tragedy or a statistic.

Was World War Two a total war?

Objectives

By the end of this lesson you will be able to:

- use *propaganda* posters as evidence
- find out what the concerns of the wartime British government were
- explain how the war affected every aspect of people's lives

One way in which governments try to communicate with people is through posters.

Getting you thinking

In every country involved in the war, the concerns of governments were the same: to persuade their people to contribute to the war effort. One way of doing this was through the use of propaganda posters.

Source A

LEAVE THIS TO US SONNY — **YOU** OUGHT TO BE OUT OF LONDON

Source B

Hitler will send no warning — so always carry your gas mask

ISSUED BY THE MINISTRY OF HOME SECURITY

MAKE-DO AND MEND says Mrs. Sew-and-Sew

Source C

Source E

Turn this RAW MATERIAL INTO WAR MATERIAL!

FURTHER INFORMATION CAN BE OBTAINED FROM :-
THE DIRECTOR of PUBLIC CLEANSING,
CITY of WESTMINSTER ·
31 CHARING CROSS ROAD, W.C.2

WOMEN OF BRITAIN COME INTO THE FACTORIES

Source D

USE SPADES NOT SHIPS

GROW YOUR OWN FOOD
AND SUPPLY YOUR OWN COOKHOUSE

Source

1 Wartime Britain depended upon imports of raw materials and food to equip and feed its armed forces, as well as the civilian population. These came by sea and had to get past U-boat attack. So any food grown at home meant less food needed to be brought by ship.

2 Gas had been used as a weapon in the trench warfare of World War One by both sides. With the heavy bombing of cities, there was a fear that gas might be used against civilian targets.

3 Whilst men were called up to fight in the armed forces their jobs still needed to be done, particularly when these jobs were concerned with making war materials. So the government needed to attract women to replace the men in the factories.

4 Making war equipment required raw materials such as metals. People were encouraged to hand in such items as saucepans or the railings around gardens. The belief was that these could be melted down and the metal reused to make into weapons.

5 With cities under threat from bombing, families were encouraged to send their children to the relative safety of the countryside. This required organisation and it was women who were targeted to do this. Childcare was seen as their traditional role and men were needed in the armed forces.

6 One of the key concerns of the wartime government was to produce the weapons and equipment the armed forces needed. This meant that factories switched from making the materials of ordinary daily life to making war materials. Civilians were encouraged to mend and repair things rather than to buy new items.

Now it's your turn

Your task is to decide what the concerns of the British government were by studying this collection of propaganda posters.
1 Match each poster to the appropriate description.
2 Give the poster a suitable short snappy caption.
3 From the evidence of these posters do you think that the British government was concerned with every aspect of people's lives? If so, can World War Two be described as a total war?

Local history

Can you find examples of garden walls where the railings have been cut off in your area? Why do you think this might have happened?

Check your progress

I can describe some features of wartime Britain.
I can describe several features of wartime Britain that the government was concerned about.
I can judge the extent to which the war affected people's everyday lives.

Propaganda: information put out by a government or other organisation to influence people's opinions

War crimes: Lidice

Many terrible things happen during wars, but trying to establish who is really responsible can be difficult.

Getting you thinking

On 27 May 1942 in Prague, in Nazi-occupied Czechoslovakia, seven men attacked a vehicle with grenades. The passenger, Reinhard Heydrich, was severely wounded and died several days later. A fortnight later, on 10 June, German soldiers entered the village of Lidice, six miles from Prague. They rounded up all 199 men and boys aged 15 or over in the village and shot them. The 60 women and 88 children were taken away. Then the village itself was completely destroyed, wiped from the face of the earth – but why?

This story begins in 1941 when Hitler appointed Heydrich as protector of Bohemia and Moravia (then regions of Czechoslovakia). Heydrich was a major figure in the Nazi plans to exterminate the Jews. In the same year, the British secret service M16 decided with the Czech resistance to assassinate Heydrich. He was the only Nazi leader deliberately targeted for assassination.

Memorial statue for the children of Lidice

On 29 December 1941 two Czech *patriots*, Jan Kubis and Josef Gabcik, were parachuted into Czechoslovakia by the Royal Air Force (RAF). They met up with the local resistance and planned the attack on Heydrich. Five months later, on 27 May, they carried it out. Three weeks later they themselves were dead. Their hiding place was betrayed and they died in a gun battle with German troops.

Patriot: someone who is proud of their country

In Germany the reaction to the assassination attempt was outrage. Some sources suggest Hitler saw Heydrich as his possible successor. Hitler wanted 30,000 Czechs killed as a reprisal, although this figure was then reduced to 10,000. That same day, 27 May, the reprisals began. Over the next few days over 3,000 Czechs were arrested, and at least 2,000 killed.

Heydrich died on 8 June and his *state funeral* was held in Berlin on 9 June. Next day Hitler ordered that a small community should be wiped out as a punishment. Lidice was chosen as one of the men who had killed Heydrich had links to the village.

After 10 June, the women and most of the children of the village were sent to concentration camps. Some of the children were considered suitable for Germanisation; that is they could become Germans by being adopted by German families. The rest were gassed to death. Sources differ in the accounts as to whether any of the women survived and, if so, how many. Meanwhile, also on 10 June, a thousand Jews were sent by train from Prague to concentration camps.

This fountain stands in Jephson Gardens in Royal Leamington Spa where Czech forces were stationed in the war. It was unveiled on the 26 October 1968, as a memorial to all the Czechs and Slovaks who died in the war and particularly to the seven Czech patriots who assassinated Heydrich.

Czech memorial in Leamington Spa

Now it's your turn

1 Construct a simple flow diagram linking each of the events in this narrative.
2 Now use your flow diagram to decide why the Lidice massacre happened.
3 Who or what do you believe was responsible for the massacre?
4 Who would you blame?
5 Sources differ on how they describe Heydrich's killers. Some call them patriots, others call them assassins. Which word would you use? Why?

Check your progress

I can construct a narrative of events.
I can explain some of causes of the massacre.
I can decide who I think was responsible for the massacre.

State funeral: special funeral, organised by the government, to honour a very important person who has died

War crimes: 'Bomber' Harris?

In 1992 a statue of Air Marshall Arthur 'Bomber' Harris was unveiled outside St Clement Danes Church in London. It had been paid for by public subscription. Some of the watching crowd booed. For weeks afterwards the statue had to be guarded from attack. In Germany some people complained that it was insensitive to make 'Bomber' Harris a hero.

Objectives

By the end of this lesson you will be able to:

- suggest some reasons for the different interpretations of 'Bomber' Harris
- explain whether 'Bomber' Harris should be commemorated with a statue

Getting you thinking

The reason for this hostility is because Harris was in charge of Bomber Command; he was the man responsible for directing the bombing of German cities, and therefore the man blamed for Dresden. To some people 'Bomber' Harris was a war criminal.

Now it's your turn

Your task is to decide if his statue should be taken down. Read through the following historical narrative and sources and decide whether Dresden was a war crime or not. If so, who, if anyone, should be held responsible?

From 1940 until 1941 the *Luftwaffe* bombed British cities. British policy was to respond by bombing German cities. This helped to maintain public morale and showed Britain's allies, particularly the Soviet Union, that Britain was making a strong contribution to the war.

In a 1941 speech Churchill said, 'We need to make the enemy burn and bleed in every way.'

Dresden after the bombing

Luftwaffe: German air force
Firestorm: an uncontrollable fire caused by bombing

On 14 February 1942, the air ministry detailed a policy change from precision bombing, hitting specific targets such as factories and railways, to area bombing – destroying whole areas of towns and cities. 'It has been decided that the primary object of your operations should now be focused on the morale of the enemy civilian population. With this aim in view, a list of selected targets … is attached.' This list included the city of Dresden.

'Bomber' Harris took over Bomber Command in 1942, and is credited with its success in destroying the industries that supplied the German armed forces. In January 1945, Albert Speer, the German minister of war production, and his officials calculated that the bombing had led to Germany producing 35 per cent fewer tanks, 31 per cent fewer aircraft, and 42 per cent fewer trucks.

Dresden

At 9.51pm on Tuesday 13 February 1945, Dresden's air raid warning sirens sounded. Minutes later the first marker flares were dropped. Weather conditions were perfect. The city was unprotected, there were no searchlights and the anti-aircraft guns had mostly been moved east to fight the advancing Soviet armies. Moreover the Nazi authorities had not built enough air raid shelters. By next morning RAF and USAAF bombers had dropped more than 4,500 tons of high explosives and incendiary bombs. This created a *firestorm* in which 25,000 people died, and that left thirteen square miles of the city centre in ruins. It was Ash Wednesday.

Statue of 'Bomber' Harris

> Dresden … was by the standards of the time a legitimate military target. The question is whether enemy cities, containing large numbers of civilians but also vital sites of manufacturing should be bombed despite the probability of high casualties among noncombatants.
>
> Frederick Taylor, 'Dresden: Tuesday 13 February 1945' (2005)

Extension work

Check figures for the death toll in the bombing of Dresden. Can you explain why they differ?

Find out how 'Bomber' Harris is described in various books or websites. What adjectives are attached to his name? Can you explain why?

Check your progress

I can suggest one reason why Dresden was/was not a war crime.

I can suggest more than one reason why Dresden was/was not a war crime.

I can suggest who was responsible for the bombing of Dresden.

Noncombatants: civilians, people who are not part of the military

War crimes: Hiroshima?

Objectives

By the end of this lesson you will be able to:

- explain why US President Truman took the decision to drop the bomb
- decide if you think its use was justified

On 6 August 1945, the American bomber Enola Gay dropped an atomic bomb on the Japanese city of Hiroshima. Within minutes, over 70,000 people were dead and as many again injured. One square mile of the city was totally destroyed. The fires that followed destroyed a further 4.4 square miles of the city. Three days later a second atomic bomb was dropped on Nagasaki and another 36,000 people died.

Getting you thinking

The decision to drop the atomic bomb was made by US President Truman who afterwards said, 'This is the greatest thing in history.' He argued that it would shorten the war, remove any need to invade Japan itself and so save the lives of thousands of American servicemen as well as Japanese civilians.

Now it's your turn

Use the fact file to help you decide if you think:
a) the facts support the claim that dropping the bomb shortened the war
b) the dropping of the atomic bomb can be justified

Alternative historical interpretations

It was not the atomic bomb but a combination of factors that led Japan to surrender.

The US wanted to drop the atomic bomb because it:
- had cost an enormous amount of money and they wanted to test it in action
- would show the USSR how powerful the USA now was

Check your progress

⭐ I can suggest one reason why the atomic bomb was dropped.
⭐⭐ I can suggest several reasons why the atomic bomb was dropped.
⭐⭐⭐ I can explain whether it was justified to drop the bomb.

The mushroom cloud from a
nuclear bomb explosion

Fact file

The city of **Hiroshima** was:
➤ a military headquarters and assembly area for troops
➤ unsuitable as an incendiary target as there were so many rivers
➤ surrounded by hills which would increase the bomb damage
➤ left deliberately untouched by US bombing planners so that the
effects of the atomic bomb could be more clearly assessed.

The **Enola Gay** was:
➤ instructed to drop the bomb only if visibility was good
➤ accompanied by another plane to photograph the explosion

US **firebombing of Japan** in 1945:
➤ 64 Japanese cities were firebombed and large areas of
them were destroyed
➤ On 9 March 1945 Tokyo was firebombed; 16 square
miles of the city were destroyed and there were
100,000 civilian casualties

The fighting in the Pacific was fierce, with high casualties when the
Americans invaded and recaptured Japanese-held islands:
Iwo Jima: Americans – 7,000 killed, 19,000 wounded
Japanese – 22,500 killed. Just 200 surrendered
Okinawa: Americans – 12,000 killed, 39,000 wounded
Japanese – 110,000 killed, plus 42-150,000 civilians killed

The US **Manhattan Project** to develop the atomic bomb:
➤ employed 130,000 people and cost US$2 billion
➤ made the first successful nuclear test on 16 July 1945

Pacific War timeline 1945

17 March	Iwo Jima captured
8 May	Germany surrendered, Japan now fighting alone
21 June	Okinawa captured, US airbase just 325 miles from Japan
17 July	Tokyo bombed by 1500 planes, which met no opposition
26 July	President Truman issued Japan with an ultimatum, surrender or else. Prime Minister Suzuki ignored this
6 August	Hiroshima atomic bomb
9 August	USSR declared war on Japan and invaded Manchuria Nagasaki atomic bomb
14 August	Japan surrendered

The Holocaust
Part 1

Objectives

By the end of this lesson you will be able to:

- describe the persecution of the Jews in Germany
- explain the role of Hitler and the Nazis in this persecution
- describe which other groups were involved

European history shows that Jews suffered attack and persecution on repeated occasions in many countries, including Germany.

Getting you thinking

Q. In which country did the following happen?
- **1189–90:** Attacks on Jews in several large cities – Jews were murdered and their homes burned.
- **1290:** The king ordered all Jews to leave.
- **1655:** Jews were officially readmitted to the country.

A. *All these events happened in England.*

In Germany *anti-Semitic* ideas were popular before Hitler and the Nazis came to power in 1933. Hitler set out his views on race in his book *Mein Kampf*; he saw Jews as an inferior race, and wanted to destroy them as part of a conspiracy to take over the world. Once he was in power, he acted against them.

- **1933:** Hitler ordered a boycott of Jewish shops. Jews were banned from teaching.
- **1935:** The Nuremberg Laws were passed. Marriage between Jews and German citizens was made illegal. Jews could not be German citizens.
- **1938:** A range of laws were passed which included banning Jewish doctors from practising.

A Jewish man clears up after 'Kristallnacht' (the 'Night of Broken Glass')

Anti-Semitism: prejudice against Jews

- **10 November 1938:** The Nazis organised attacks on Jewish synagogues and properties. Over a thousand Jews were killed and so many windows were smashed that the event was called 'Kristallnacht' (the 'Night of Broken Glass').
- **1938:** Further laws added more restrictions, such as banning Jews from running businesses, going to cinemas, driving cars and sending their children to school.

All this made life increasingly difficult for Germany's 500,000 Jews. Many tried to leave or send their children abroad (see pages 78–79). Things worsened in 1939 when war broke out. First the German armies conquered Poland, where many Jews lived. Then in 1941 Germany invaded the Soviet Union, bringing the number of Jews living in German-occupied territory to over six million. Following behind the German armies were the SS units, whose job it was to find and kill Jews. This is seen as the starting point of the *Holocaust*.

What was the Holocaust?

Here is the definition from Yad Vashem, the Jewish people's living memorial to the Holocaust in Jerusalem, Israel:

> 'The Holocaust was the murder of approximately six million Jews by the Nazis and their collaborators. Between the German invasion of the Soviet Union in the summer of 1941 and the end of the war in Europe in May 1945, Nazi Germany and its accomplices strove to murder every Jew under their control. Because Nazi discrimination against the Jews began with Hitler's accession to power in January 1933, many historians consider this the start of the Holocaust era. The Jews were not the only victims of Hitler's regime, but they were the only group that the Nazis sought to destroy entirely.'

The other victims were gypsies, homosexuals, Jehovah's Witnesses, mentally or physically disabled people, political opponents, prisoners of war and slave labourers taken from German-occupied countries.

Now it's your turn

Prepare a short presentation explaining the events leading up to the Holocaust. Where would you place its starting point?

Check your progress

I can describe one way in which German Jews were persecuted.
I can describe the events leading up to the start of the Holocaust.
I can explain the role of Hitler and the Nazis in these events.

Holocaust: a biblical word for sacrifice
Collaborators: people from other nations who helped the Nazis

The Holocaust
Part 2

Having looked at the origins of the Holocaust, we will now look at what happened.

Getting you thinking

In 1942 the shooting of Jews was replaced by a new method, gassing. The Nazis had used concentration camps to hold their enemies but now new camps were built. These were 'death camps', where the Jews would be killed. All six of these were built in Poland, in locations chosen for their good rail links and relative isolation. Jews from German-occupied countries all over Europe were to be rounded up, sent there by train and gassed to death.

Auschwitz today

Now it's your turn

Within this 'big picture' there are thousands of portraits and stories of individuals. The roles of these individuals have been categorised as victims, resistors, *perpetrators*, collaborators, bystanders and rescuers.

Your task is to decide into which category each of the following people fit.

Perpetrator: someone who carries out an act

One after the other, they had to remove their luggage, then their coats, shoes, and over garments and also underwear ... Once undressed, they were led into the ravine ... When they reached the bottom they were seized by members of the *Schutzpolizei* and made to lie down on top of Jews who had already been shot ... The corpses were literally in layers. A police marksman came along and shot each Jew in the neck with a submachine gun.

Source 1 *Truck driver, Kiev, September 1941*

Every morning we were woken to attend roll call. ... We had to go outside and line up. We had to stand like this until every single inmate of the camp had been counted. This included all those who had died during the night. Sometimes this would take up to five hours. You can imagine how we felt in the middle of winter. The people in my hut used to help one another. We would stand as close to the person in front as we could and then we would use our warm breath to breathe on the back of their necks. So you see we were beating the Nazis yet again. We kept our humanity.

Source 3 *Regina Scherer, Auschwitz survivor*

Another improvement we made over Treblinka was that we built our gas chambers to accommodate 2,000 people at one time. The way we selected our victims was as follows: we had two SS doctors on duty at Auschwitz to examine the incoming transports of prisoners. The prisoners would be marched by one of the doctors who would make spot decisions as they walked by. Those who were fit for work were sent into the camp. Others were sent immediately to the extermination plants. Children of tender years were invariably exterminated, since by reason of their youth they were unable to work.

Source 2 *Rudolf Höss, Auschwitz camp commandant, testifying at Nuremberg*

In September there were rumours that the Germans intended to deport all Denmark's 7,000 Jews. One, scientist Niels Bohr, escaped to Sweden to ask for help. The Swedish government agreed. The day before the round up, most of Denmark's Jews were smuggled by Danish fishermen to neutral Sweden.

'At Sobibor death camp on October 13 six hundred Jewish slave labourers were being forced to dig up and burn the bodies of those killed in 1942. Armed with knives and hatchets they attacked their guards, killed nine SS men and two Ukrainians. About one hundred escaped to the forests and joined partisan groups fighting the Germans. The rest were shot.

Source 4 *Two 1943 incidents recounted by historian Martin Gilbert*

Check your progress

I can describe individual experiences of the Holocaust.
I can categorise individuals as victims, resistors, perpetrators, collaborators, bystanders or rescuers.
I can say why I have put individuals into a particular category.

The Holocaust
Part 3

Objectives

By the end of this lesson you will be able to:

- explain why some Jews survived the Holocaust
- explore some of the reasons why the Holocaust should be studied

The Nazis called the killing of the Jews the 'final solution'. They planned to wipe out the Jews of Europe. However, although they killed over six million Jewish people, the Nazis and their collaborators did not kill them all.

Getting you thinking

When the war ended in 1945, some of the Jews imprisoned in the camps were still alive. Others emerged from where they had been hidden by non-Jews; some had already made their escape before the Nazi invaders had arrived. Many survivors of the Holocaust went to live in what was to become the modern state of Israel. Whether a Jewish person survived depended very much on where they lived in 1939, as the table below shows.

Country	Jewish population before 1939	Percentage who died, 1939–1945
Denmark	7,000	<1
France	350,000	26
Germany	350,000	90
Poland	3,300,000	90

Can you suggest reasons why the percentage of the Jewish population who died was so different between these four countries?

Below left: Child prisoners in Auschwitz

Below right: Shoes belonging to victims of the Nazi death camp, Auschwitz

Now it's your turn

The British government has made it a legal requirement for all secondary schools to teach students about the Holocaust. In 2001 Holocaust Memorial Day was introduced. This is commemorated on 27 January every year.

On the right are a number of reasons why the Holocaust should be studied. They come from a guide for teachers published by *The Task Force for International Cooperation on Holocaust Education, Remembrance and Research.*

Which do you find most convincing and why?

The historian Martin Gilbert has written this judgement on the Holocaust:

> *... it depended most of all, one survivor has remarked, 'upon the indifference of bystanders in every land'.*

Which one of the reasons A–E do you think he would choose?

A The Holocaust was a watershed event, not only for the 20th century but also in the entire history of humanity. It was an unprecedented attempt to murder a whole people and to extinguish its culture. The Holocaust should be studied because it fundamentally challenged the foundations of civilisation.

B A thorough study of the Holocaust helps students think about the use and abuse of power, and the roles and responsibilities of individuals, organisations, and nations when confronted with human rights violations. It can heighten awareness of the potential for genocide in the contemporary world.

C Studying the Holocaust assists students in developing an understanding of prejudice, racism, anti-Semitism, and stereotyping in any society. It helps students develop an awareness of the value of diversity in a pluralistic society and encourages sensitivity to the positions of minorities.

D The Holocaust provides a context for exploring the dangers of remaining silent and indifferent in the face of the oppression of others.

E The Holocaust has become a central theme in the culture of many countries. This is reflected in media representation and popular culture. Holocaust education can offer students historical knowledge and skills needed to understand and evaluate these.

Check your progress

I can describe how Jews were treated differently in different countries.

I can explain why the Holocaust is studied.

I can reach a judgement on the most important reasons why the Holocaust should be studied.

Bystander: someone who stands by and observes but is not involved in an event

Comparison: World War One and World War Two

Objectives

By the end of this lesson you will be able to:

- describe some of the similarities and differences between the two World Wars
- explain how some changes altered the nature of warfare

Getting you thinking

Compare the two RAF fighter planes in the photographs. What differences can you see or work out from the photographs and the caption?

Air warfare became important in World War One. To begin with, aircraft were used for *reconnaissance*, to find out what the enemy were doing. Later these aircraft were armed, so that they could defend themselves and attack enemy reconnaissance aircraft. These were the first fighter planes, and included the Sopwith Camel. Battles or 'dogfights' took place between them, as each side tried to gain control of the airspace above battlegrounds. The exploits of fighter pilots caught the public imagination and the cult of the 'ace' was born; high 'scoring' pilots such as Albert Ball and Manfred von Richthofen ('The Red Baron') became famous. Air support for ground operations was also developed, with the bombing and *strafing* of enemy troops and transport. In the later stages of the war, small-scale airdrops of supplies to ground units were started.

Alongside fighter planes, bomber aircraft were also developed to bomb troops that were out of artillery range. All sides bombed military targets but opinions were divided on whether it was acceptable to bomb cities. This was a tactic that Germany adopted, first using zeppelins and then Gotha bombers. There were 4,822 British civilian casualties, of whom 1,413 were killed. The Germans' intention was to *demoralise* civilian populations. Despite the moral debate, both sides did bomb cities.

An RAF Sopwith Camel fighter, 1917.
Max speed 115mph.
Armament 2 x Vickers machine guns.
Range 485 km.
Ceiling 6,400m.

Reconnaissance: exploring an area to gather military information
Strafing: attacking targets on the ground from low-flying aircraft

An RAF Gloster Meteor fighter, 1945.
Max speed 410mph.
Armament 4 x British Hispano cannons.
Range 800 km.
Ceiling 11,500m.

During World War Two, aircraft became increasingly important. They were faster, better armed and had a longer range. This led to increased use in ground support, such as the German 'Blitzkrieg' tactics. They were also used to attack ships and submarines. Fighters continued to be improved, culminating in the introduction of jet aircraft by both Britain and Germany in 1944, and of German rocket–powered missiles, the V1 and V2. The cult of the fighter 'ace' continued with pilots such as Johnnie Johnson and Adolf Gallant.

Bombers were also more technologically advanced. They were used for strategic bombing, attacking targets well beyond the battlefield, such as factories, transport networks and centres of government and population. Examples include the German Blitz on Britain (1940-41), the British and American raids on Germany (see pages 112-113), and the American raids on Japan. These attacks inevitably caused high numbers of civilian deaths; in Britain there were over 60,000 civilian casualties. In other combatant nations, civilian deaths from bombing were even higher. The *morality* of such tactics was questioned at the time and is still a matter of debate today.

Now it's your turn

1 How did warfare change between World War One and World War Two?
2 How did warfare stay the same?
3 Would you agree that improved technology led to 'total war'?

Check your progress

I can describe some differences between World War One and World War Two.
I can explain some of the changes in warfare.
I can appreciate the way in which the nature of warfare changed between the two world wars.

Demoralise: destroy confidence, cause chaos
Morality: rightness, acceptability

D-Day

D–Day, 6 June 1944, was the day the Allied powers invaded Nazi-controlled Europe. Several Hollywood filmmakers have told the story of the landings.

Getting you thinking

Saving Private Ryan (1998) by Stephen Spielberg was inspired by the true story of four brothers, three of whom were in Normandy on D-Day. Sergeant Robert Niland, 505th Parachute Regiment, was killed near Neuville; his older brother, Second Lieutenant Preston Niland, 22nd Infantry Regiment, was killed on Utah Beach. Meanwhile, the eldest brother Sergeant Edward Niland, US Army Air Force, was missing presumed dead after his bomber was shot down over Burma in May*. Their mother received three telegrams from the US War Department announcing their deaths on the same day.

The army wanted to make sure that she would not lose another son. So an army chaplain escorted the fourth and youngest brother, Sergeant Frederick 'Fritz' Niland, 501st Parachute Regiment, out of the front line in Normandy. Fritz was sent back to the USA.

Commenting on the film, the historian Stephen Ambrose, author of 'D-Day, June 6, 1944: The Climactic Battle of World War II' (1994), said: 'I don't think the Army would have sent out a squad to look for one guy. Now there is this kernel of truth [in the film as] to the story of Fritz Niland, but they found him right away and flew him out.'

So if the filmmakers have made one change for the dramatic purposes of the plot, have they made others?

Filmmakers are not historians. They make films to entertain rather than to educate people. However, their films are very persuasive and many people regard them as true accounts of what actually happened!

* Ironically, Edward Niland parachuted safely to ground, was captured and spent the war in a Japanese prisoner of war camp. So he, too, survived.

Source 1 *Advertising poster: 'Saving Private Ryan'*

Source 2 *Advertising poster: ' 'The Longest Day'*

The Longest Day (1962) is Hollywood's definitive D-Day movie. More modern accounts such as *Saving Private Ryan* are more vividly realistic, but producer Darryl F Zanuck's epic 1962 account is the only one to attempt the daunting task of covering that fateful day from all perspectives. From the German High Command and front-line officers to the French Resistance and all the key Allied participants …

Source 3 *Extract from the Amazon website description*

There have been many previous attempts to recreate the D-Day landings on screen … but thanks to Spielberg's freewheeling hand-held camerawork, Ryan was the first time an audience really felt like they were there, storming up Omaha Beach in the face of withering enemy fire. … Some non-US critics have complained that Ryan portrays only the American D-Day experience, but it is an American film made and financed by Americans, after all.

Source 4 *Extract from the Amazon website description*

British 2nd Army

83,000 men in total, 60 000 British, over 20,000 Canadian, plus Free French

American First Army

73,000 men in total

Source 5 *Allied forces on D-day*

Now it's your turn

1 Study sources 1 and 2. What nationality are the men depicted?
2 What is the strength of *Saving Private Ryan*?
3 What are the historical weaknesses of the film?
4 Now consider *The Longest Day*. What key omission can you find?
5 Is it fair to say that we should take care not to believe how Hollywood films depict the past?

Check your progress

I can explore features of historical interpretations.
I can compare how different filmmakers have depicted D-Day.
I can suggest reasons why filmmakers' interpretations of D-Day differ.

Was Victory in Europe (VE) Day the same for everyone?

In Britain, Victory in Europe (VE) Day was 8 May 1945, the date when the Allies accepted the unconditional surrender of the German armed forces.

Getting you thinking

The photograph below shows some of the million people who came out onto the streets in Britain to celebrate the end of the war, and the Allies' victory. Choose one individual from the picture and think about why VE Day may have been a cause for celebration for them.

World wars, like any other complex historical event, do not end neatly. The fighting and dying went on right up to the very last minute. On 7 May a German U-boat sank two merchant ships off Scotland. Whilst Germany's military leaders formally surrendered on that day, some German units had surrendered earlier, and others continued to fight the Red Army for several more days.

Rejoicing crowds in Piccadilly, London on VE Day, 1945

Austerity: shortages of food and clothes, no luxuries, 'belt-tightening'
Kamikaze: suicide bomber

In Britain, individuals reacted in different ways. Some celebrated at one of the many street parties; others spent the day in quiet reflection. Many were too busy working to do either. The country was war-weary; there had been years of *austerity* and rationing, which would continue into the 1950s. Half a million homes had been destroyed. Many millions of lives were disrupted and the casualty figures were high.

British forces in Germany celebrated but some were still close to German troops who did not believe that the war was over, so they had to carry on as usual. Many individuals felt a sense of relief that they had survived, tinged with sadness at the deaths of friends. There was also the war in the Far East to consider. Fighting still continued against the Japanese and being posted to that theatre of war was a real possibility. The forces in the Far East had nothing to celebrate; the day after VE Day the aircraft carrier HMS Victorious was hit by a Japanese *kamikaze* plane.

Eastern Europe, which was on Moscow time, celebrated VE day on 9 May. But not everyone celebrated. In Poland it marked the day the Poles lost their freedom. In 1939 Poland had been invaded both by Nazi Germany and by the Soviet Union. On VE day it was still occupied by the Red Army. Post-war Poland was smaller and its borders had been moved westwards.

Poland was ruled by the Communist Party, backed by Soviet military power. As a result, many Poles who had fought with the British chose not to go home. Out of around 265,000 Polish armed forces in the West in 1945, just 105,000 returned to Poland, while 160,000 stayed, mostly in Britain.

Poland and its neighbours in 1939 and 1945. The green area shows the overlap between the Poland of 1939 and 1945

There was also the Katyn Massacre: in 1940 roughly 20,000 Polish officers and *intellectuals* captured by the Red Army disappeared inside the Soviet Union. In 1943 advancing German armies uncovered 4,500 corpses in the forest of Katyn; the rest were never found. It was not until the 1990s, after the collapse of Communist rule, that ordinary Poles were able to state openly that the Red Army had committed the murders on Stalin's orders.

Now it's your turn

1 How did British people's experience of VE Day differ?
2 How did Polish people's experience of VE Day differ?

Check your progress

I can describe some differences in people's experience of VE Day.
I can explain some of the differences.
I can reach a conclusion about the nature of diversity.

Intellectuals: people who work with their minds, thinkers

What happened at Nuremberg?

At the end of the war the Allies met to plan what should happen next. One issue to resolve was how to treat war criminals. They decided to set up an International Criminal Court in Nuremberg. Nuremberg was chosen because the court buildings were large enough and relatively undamaged by Allied bombing. There was also a large prison to hold the *defendants*. Nuremberg was the site of the annual Nazi Party rallies and so, symbolically, a good place to bring Nazism to an end.

Getting you thinking

Study the picture. What do you think the roles of the different groups of people are?

Hermann Goering, Rudolf Hess, Joachim von Ribbentrop and Wilhelm Keitel at the Nuremberg Trials, 1945-46

Defendants: *those charged with crimes*
Ballistic missiles: missiles that are guided at start but fall freely towards their targets

The trials took place from 1945-49. The major war criminals were tried first, followed by others, such as members of the extermination squads and doctors from the death camps. Not all Nazi leaders were tried; some, like Hitler, committed suicide in the last days of the war. Others were killed and some escaped.

The 21 men whose trial began on 20 November 1945 included leading Nazi politicians and military leaders, notably Hermann Goering (commander of the Luftwaffe), Rudolf Hess (deputy leader until 1943) and Albert Speer (minister of Armaments).

They were accused on one or more of four charges:
- Conspiring to wage war
- Planning and waging wars of aggression and committing other crimes against peace
- Crimes against humanity (including the newly defined crime of genocide)
- War crimes (abuse and murder of prisoners, use of slave labour and killing of civilians).

Of those convicted, eleven were sentenced to death; the rest were sentenced to imprisonment.

Nuremberg is seen as significant because it set a precedent for future conflicts. The International Court of Justice at The Hague is its modern descendent. But not everyone agreed that Nuremberg was legal. There were also those who believed that other war criminals should have been prosecuted. These included war criminals of other nationalities, such as those responsible for the Katyn massacres. They also included some Germans who were protected by the Allies because of their scientific knowledge.

One example was Werner von Braun. He worked on developing the V2 rockets that were used to attack Britain from September 1944. Over 5,000 were launched at London, killing 2,700 people and injuring 6,000. At the end of the war he surrendered to US forces. He and forty other rocket scientists were then moved to the USA where they began new lives and worked on developing *ballistic missiles*. Braun also worked on the space programme, developing the Saturn rocket that took men to the moon in 1969.

Now it's your turn

1 Who was tried at Nuremberg?
2 Who was not tried at Nuremberg and why?

Check your progress

I can list the names of some people who were tried and some who were not tried at Nuremberg.

I can explain why not everyone faced trial.

I can decide which kind of court should try war criminals, and give reasons.

Extension work

In 1945 some people criticised the International Criminal Court, saying it was just the victors handing out rough justice. They believed that war criminals should be dealt with by their own country.

Think about this question in the light of the International Court of Justice at The Hague.

Do you think those accused of crimes against humanity should be tried by an international court, or should they be tried in their own country?

What sort of war was World War Two?

Aerial warfare in World War Two

You have been studying various aspects of World War Two. Now you are going to carry out a task that will help you to check your progress. Read the instructions very carefully. They tell you what to do, how to plan your task and how to assess your work.

Assessment task

You are going to prepare for a class debate on the question, 'What sort of war was World War Two?'

1 Think back over the various aspects of World War Two that you have studied in this unit.

2 Compare each of these to the following possible descriptions of the war. World War Two was:
- Hitler's war
- a global war
- a total war
- a war of tragedies or courage
- a war of war crimes
- a war of turning points
- a million different wars

3 Choose which description you think is most appropriate.

4 Make a list of the evidence or historical details which support your choice.

5 Use this list to prepare a one-minute presentation justifying your choice. Make sure that you state your position clearly and that you support your claim with evidence, historical details and historical explanation.

6 Rehearse your presentation and make any final adjustments needed.

Check your level

I can describe one characteristic feature of World War Two.	I can describe several features of World War Two.	I can describe the diverse features of World War Two.
I can support my answer with evidence, historical knowledge or explanations.	I can use a range of evidence, historical knowledge or explanation to support my answer.	I can select from a range of evidence, historical knowledge or explanations to support my answer.
I can use historical terms in my presentation.	I can use historical terms to help make my ideas clear and my presentation interesting.	I can use historical terms to help make my presentation clear and convincing.
Level **5**	Level **6**	Level **7**

The world after 1945

Objectives

By the end of this unit you will be able to:

- compare the relative significance of historic developments and systems of belief

In 1945 America was the richest and most powerful country in the world. It went into the 21st century as the only remaining superpower. Many Americans, however, have never taken all this for granted – but why not?

Nuclear bomb test, Bikini and Enewetak Atolls, 21 October 1952

Mourners in Wootton Bassett stand silently as hearses carrying the bodies of British soldiers killed in Afghanistan pass down the high street, Febuary 2010

Look at the photographs. The large one shows the mushroom cloud of a nuclear explosion, the smaller one a recent funeral procession in Wootton Bassett in England.

On 6 August 1945, America dropped an atomic bomb on the Japanese city of Hiroshima, killing 80,000 people instantly. Within decades, the US and its opponent, the Soviet Union, were armed with enough nuclear weapons to destroy the earth seventeen times over. In 1962 and 1983 the two sides came very close to nuclear war. The United Kingdom, an ally of the US, also has nuclear weapons.

Americans have also always felt threatened by powerful ideas that seem the enemies of their own. Communism (represented by the Soviet Union and sometimes China) was seen as the chief threat until 1989. Since the attack on New York in 2001, America has waged what was called a 'War on Terror' against terrorists from the Islamic world who see the United States as their enemy. The 'War on Terror' included an invasion of Afghanistan in 2002; British soldiers were still being killed there in 2010, fighting as allies of America.

Questions

Create a set of 'threats to the USA' cards with the following separate headings:

- Destruction through nuclear war (1949–1989)
- Chinese economic growth in the 21st century
- Chinese military spending in the 21st century
- Take-over of the world by communism (1945–1989)
- Take-over of the Muslim world by terrorists (from 2001)
- Attacks by terrorists from the Muslim world (1993–present)
- Nuclear weapons development by Iran (future)
- Return of Russia to dictatorship

With a partner arrange these by order of importance, taking into account how long the threat lasted or might last, and how dangerous a threat it was or appears to be.

When did Americans feel most threatened by the Soviet Union from 1946 to 1960?

Objectives

By the end of this lesson you will be able to:

- use evidence to suggest when Americans felt most threatened by the Soviet Union between 1946 and 1960

We have seen how Germany surrendered in 1945. The country was divided up by the wartime Allies, who shared a determination never to let Germany threaten peace again. But how long could an alliance formed with Hitler as a common enemy survive?

Getting you thinking

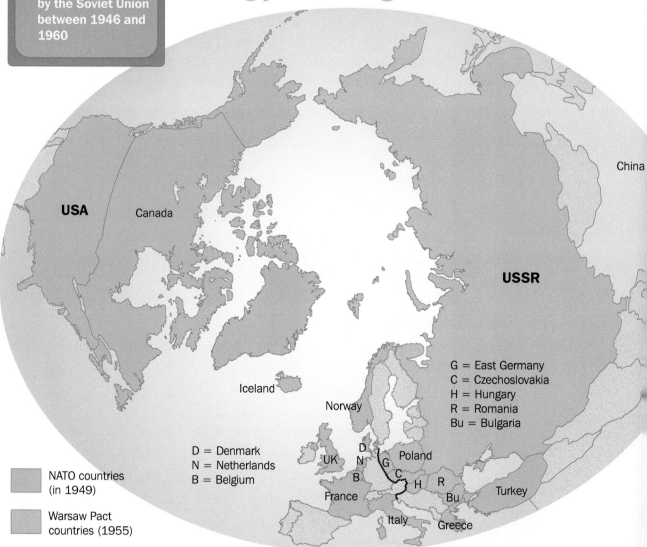

G = East Germany
C = Czechoslovakia
H = Hungary
R = Romania
Bu = Bulgaria

D = Denmark
N = Netherlands
B = Belgium

NATO countries (in 1949)

Warsaw Pact countries (1955)

The Cold War world

- How many countries are coloured blue on the map?
- How many are coloured red?
- Which appear to be the largest countries on each side?

North Atlantic Treaty Organisation (NATO): a Western organisation set up in 1949 to promote collective security during the Cold War

By 1950, Europe was divided into two. Ordinary Americans had been sick of war by 1945, but their leaders were suspicious of Stalin. Between 1945 and 1948 Stalin's communist supporters took over Eastern Europe. To deter further Soviet expansion, US President Truman formed the *North Atlantic Treaty Organisation* (NATO) in January 1949, an alliance of the blue countries on the map. In August 1949, however, Americans were shocked and alarmed; Stalin's scientists exploded the first Soviet atomic bomb, with secrets stolen from the US. Then in October 1949 China became communist too. In 1955, to rival NATO, Stalin and his Eastern European allies formed the *Warsaw Pact*.

NATO and the Warsaw Pact were not at war with each other – yet. Instead they fought a 'cold war' by building up weapons, spying on each other and supporting allies who fought on their behalf.

The table on the right shows what happened between 1950 and 1960, what Americans were told about it, and what American presidents secretly knew or thought.

Now it's your turn

1 Draw a graph. Along the bottom, mark the years 1946 to 1960. Down the side at the bottom put 'not threatened at all', half way up the side put 'quite threatened', and at the top 'really threatened'. Plot onto the graph events that you decide made the Americans feel more or less threatened by the Soviet Union.

2 When did the Americans feel most and least threatened?

3 Why was this?

What happened 1950–1960

- In 1950 Stalin ordered his ally North Korea to invade America's ally, South Korea. The UN, led by America, fought a bitter war against North Korea (which was supported by Chinese communists). The war ended in 1953 with no borders changed.
- In 1953 Stalin died.
- In 1956, Hungarian leaders tried to give more freedom to their people. The Soviet Union invaded and occupied Hungary. The US criticised the invasion.
- In 1957 the Soviet Union put Sputnik, the first satellite, into space.
- In 1959 the Cuban government was overthrown by a pro-communist revolution. Cuba is only 180km from the American state of Florida.

What Americans were told by their government and media

- The Soviet Union wanted to spread communism throughout the world by force. It had to be 'contained' by the US.
- From 1948 to 1954, US Senator McCarthy accused many important Americans of being communist spies.
- America was falling behind Soviet technology.
- Through the 1950s, the Soviets were building more and more nuclear missiles, closing the gap with the US.

What American presidents secretly knew or thought

- US President Eisenhower (1952–1960) disliked Senator McCarthy. However, McCarthy was too popular to criticise in public.
- US and Soviet warplanes actually fought each other during the Korean War. The Americans shot down more Soviet warplanes.
- The US would not risk nuclear war to help the Hungarians in 1956.
- The Soviets did not have as many missiles as they claimed. They were not catching up with the US.

Check your progress

I can plot the graph.
I can decide when the Americans felt most and least threatened.
I can explain why the Americans felt more or less threatened.

Warsaw Pact: an East European organisation set up in 1955 to promote collective security during the Cold War

When did Americans feel mos threatened by the Soviet Unio from 1960 to 1976?

Objectives

By the end of this lesson you will be able to:

- use evidence to suggest when Americans felt most threatened by the Soviet Union from 1960 to 1976

In 1960 President John F. Kennedy was elected president of the United States. He was young, attractive and popular – but would he make a fresh start with the Soviet Union?

Getting you thinking

Vietnam

Laos

Cambodia

Burma

Malaysia

The US feared that if any of these Asian countries fell to communism, the others might follow.

- Why are these countries lined up as a row of dominoes in the diagram? What would happen if you pushed over South Vietnam according to this diagram?
- Locate these countries in an atlas. How close are they together?

The table on the right shows what happened between 1960 and 1976, what Americans were told about this, and what American presidents secretly knew or thought.

What happened 1960–1976

- In 1961 war nearly broke out between NATO and the Warsaw Pact in Berlin. In 1962 the Soviets sent missiles to their ally Cuba and war very nearly broke out again. The Soviet Union withdrew its missiles from Cuba.
- From 1965, American soldiers fought communist North Vietnamese *guerrillas* to protect US ally, South Vietnam.
- In 1968, the Soviet Union invaded its ally, Czechoslovakia to stop Czech leaders from giving more freedom to their people.
- From the late 1960s, the US was struggling to win the Vietnam War, which was very unpopular with many Americans.
- In 1973, the US agreed to withdraw its troops from South Vietnam and signed a treaty with the Soviet Union called SALT I, limiting the number of nuclear weapons for the first time. This 'thaw' in the Cold War was called 'détente' – meaning a loosening of tension. Relations between the US and the Soviet Union improved.
- Despite détente, the Soviets still supported communists who took over: Ethiopia in Africa (1974); South Vietnam, Laos and Cambodia in Asia; Angola and Mozambique in Africa (1975)
- In 1975 the US, Soviet Union and other countries signed the Helsinki Agreement; part of the agreement said that all the governments who signed it would respect human rights.

What American were told by their presidents and media

- In 1962, the USA forced the Soviet Union to back down and withdraw its missiles from Cuba.
- The US had to support South Vietnam, otherwise other countries would fall to communism like row of dominoes.
- During the 1960s and 1970s, the US and Soviet Union had so many nuclear weapons between them, neither side would dare to risk a direct war with each other. This was called M.A.D. – mutually assured destruction.
- The US **chose** to withdraw from Vietnam in 1973 – its army was never defeated by the North Vietnamese communists.
- The SALT I Treaty would improve relations with the Soviet Union making nuclear war less likely.

What American presidents secretly knew or thought

- President Kennedy agreed a secret deal with the Soviets over Cuba in 1961. In return for the Soviet Union withdrawing its missiles from Cuba, he agreed to withdraw American missiles from Turkey and not to invade Cuba.
- President Nixon realised that the Vietnam War was very unpopular and could probably not be won. He cut his losses and withdrew, knowing it was possible South Vietnam and other countries might become communist.

Now it's your turn

1 Draw a graph. Along the bottom, put the years 1960 to 1976. Down the side at the bottom put 'not threatened at all', half way up the side put 'quite threatened', and at the top 'really threatened'. Plot on events you decide made the Americans feel more or less threatened by the Soviet Union.
2 When do you think the Americans would have felt most and least threatened?
3 Why was this?

Check your progress

⋆ I can plot a graph showing when the Americans felt threatened by the Soviet Union between 1960 and 1976.
⋆⋆ I can decide when the Americans felt most threatened.
⋆⋆⋆ I can explain why the Americans felt threatened.

When did Americans feel threatened by the Soviet Union from 1976 to 1980?

Objectives

By the end of this lesson you will be able to:

- use evidence to suggest when Americans felt most and least threatened by the Soviet Union between 1976 and 1980

We have seen that both sides clashed over certain 'hotspot countries' during the Cold War, such as Korea or Vietnam. At the end of the 1970s, the Soviet Union decided to risk a 'Vietnam War' of its own.

Getting you thinking

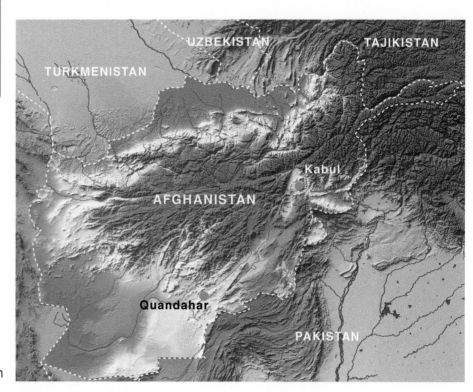

Relief map of Afghanistan

Study the map of Afghanistan.

- How much of the country is made up of mountains?
- Why might this make life hard for invaders?

On 25 December 1979, politicians and ordinary people in Europe and North America were relaxing over the Christmas holiday. Meanwhile, thousands of Soviet tanks poured over the border into Afghanistan. Within two days, Soviet commandos had seized the radio and television stations and stormed the presidential palace, killing the president and his sons. 5,000 Soviet 'advisers' took over government offices in the capital city, Kabul; Soviet military police calmly directed traffic. In January returning Soviet soldiers were greeted in Moscow

Mujahadeen: Afghan rebels who fought the Soviets

with medals and flowers. The Red Army had put a more reliable, pro-Soviet, communist government in power. All it thought its soldiers had to do was keep the peace.

US president Jimmy Carter called the invasion 'the most serious threat to peace since the Second World War'. One of his advisers wanted to make the Soviet Union 'bleed' for what it had done. The Americans thought this was the Soviet Union's first step towards a take-over of the rich oilfields of the Middle East, on which the US and its allies relied for their energy.

The US government promptly:
- shelved a new SALT II Treaty with the Soviet Union that would have further limited nuclear weapons on both sides
- increased American spending on weapons
- sent money to Afghan rebels to buy weapons to attack Soviet forces
- encouraged rich American allies like Saudi Arabia (a Muslim country) to fund the rebels

These Afghan rebels were called the *Mujahadeen*. United by Islam, they were fighting a holy war for *Allah* (God) against godless, foreign invaders. By the end of 1980, around 125,000 Soviet soldiers were *pinned down* in Afghanistan. Troops were killed, convoys attacked and casualties rose. The rebels easily melted back into their mountains. Commentators started comparing Afghanistan to Vietnam. But how had détente come to this?

From his election in 1977, President Jimmy Carter annoyed the Soviets by criticising their human rights record. Claiming that the Soviets were breaking the Helsinki Agreement, Carter provided support for people protesting about the arrest and treatment of those who disagreed with communist rule, both within the Soviet Union and in other communist countries. The Soviets mistrusted Carter and introduced new SS-20 missiles into Eastern Europe, directed towards Western Europe. In response, Carter sited 464 new cruise missiles in Western Europe in 1978. That same year, communists took over Afghanistan. The Cold War was back on.

Now it's your turn

1 Draw a graph marking 1976 to 1980 along the bottom. Down the side at the bottom put 'not threatened at all', half way up 'quite threatened', and at the top 'really threatened'. Plot events or factors you think made the Americans feel more or less threatened by the Soviet Union.
2 When did the Americans feel most and least threatened?
3 Why was this?

Check your progress

⭐ I can complete a graph showing when the Americans felt threatened by the Soviet Union between 1976 and 1980.

⭐⭐ I can decide when the Americans felt most and least threatened.

⭐⭐⭐ I can explain why the Americans felt threatened.

Allah: Muslim term for God
Pinned down: military term for a unit that is being suppressed by enemy fire

Did Ronald Reagan really end the Cold War?

Objectives

By the end of this lesson you will be able to:

- select evidence to support a specific historical interpretation
- suggest what kind of evidence could be used to argue against an interpretation

In January 1981, 70-year-old Ronald Reagan became the oldest ever US president. He claimed 'America has lost faith in itself ... we have to recapture our dreams, our pride in ourselves and our country.' But how would he do this?

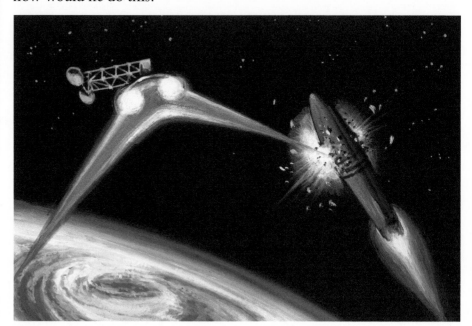

Reagan's Strategic Defense Initiative (SDI)

Getting you thinking

Look at the picture.

- Where does this seem to be taking place?
- What appears to be happening to the missile?

Within two weeks of Reagan taking office, defence spending rose by over $30 billion dollars; it increased by 50 per cent in his first term as president. He wanted to show the Soviets that they could not outspend the US. He said 'as far as an arms race is concerned, there's one going on right now, but there's only one side racing'. Reagan was not content to 'contain' communism – he wanted to roll it back. He:

- supported the independent trade union, Solidarity, against the communist party in Poland
- sent arms to forces in other countries fighting pro-Soviet groups or governments including Afghanistan
- invaded and overthrew the pro-communist government of Grenada in the Caribbean in 1983

In 1983 Reagan called the Soviet Union 'an evil empire'. He poured millions of dollars into researching his Strategic Defense Initiative (SDI), nicknamed 'Star Wars'. Lasers in space would shoot down any incoming Soviet missile over North America. If 'Star Wars' was ever built, the US could risk a nuclear war without worrying that both sides would be destroyed.

In 1985 a new and younger Soviet leader, Mikhail Gorbachev, came to power in Moscow. He knew the Soviet Union could not outspend the US. Between 1985 and 1989, Ronald Reagan negotiated with him to cut back weapons on both sides. In 1987 Reagan visited Berlin with Gorbachev and urged him to 'tear down' the Berlin Wall (a communist barrier across the city that stopped East Germans escaping to West Berlin, an area which had been controlled by the Americans, British and French since 1945). Reagan finished his time as president in January 1989. Later that year the Berlin Wall was pulled down; the communist countries of Eastern Europe became democratic and Soviet soldiers left Afghanistan.

Reagan died in 2004. His friend, former British prime minister Margaret Thatcher, said, 'Ronald Reagan had a higher claim than any other leader to have won the Cold War … and he did it without firing a shot … a truly great American hero'.

Lou Cannon, Reagan's biographer said, 'He certainly didn't end the Cold War by himself, but he led the way. The military build-up he started, and Soviet concerns about SDI, made it possible for him to negotiate from a position of strength.'

Now it's your turn

In 2001 the US Navy named a new aircraft carrier after Ronald Reagan. In this activity, imagine that you are an American official in 2001 recommending that this should happen.

1 Decide on any information from these pages you think might be useful to prove that Ronald Reagan deserves this honour. Turn this into a mind map.
2 Write up a report recommending that the aircraft carrier should be named after Reagan.
3 What kind of information might you need to argue against what you have written for question 2?

Badge of USS Ronald Reagan

Check your progress

I can complete a mind map of useful information.
I can write a report in favour of naming an aircraft carrier after Ronald Reagan.
I can suggest what kind of information I might need to argue against the recommendations in my report.

What does the story of the Berlin Wall reveal?

Objectives

By the end of this lesson you will be able to:

- suggest what the story of the Berlin Wall reveals about its significance

After Nazi Germany surrendered in 1945, the German capital Berlin was divided into four occupation zones. The Americans, British and French controlled West Berlin, while in 1950 the Soviets declared their zone of East Berlin as the capital of communist East Germany. How could the city ever be reunited?

Getting you thinking

Look at the picture.
- What are the people doing to the wall?
- Who is trying to stop them?

West Berlin became a modern, democratic Western European city totally surrounded by the drab territory of a communist state. East Germany was a ruthless dictatorship. Large numbers of ordinary people spied on their neighbours for the secret police (the Stasi). Living standards were low and many East Germans escaped to West Berlin. East German leaders asked Soviet leader, Nikita Khrushchev, what to do. He suggested building a barrier around West Berlin to prevent East Germans from escaping. Under cover of darkness on Sunday 13 August 1961, workmen under armed guard drove concrete posts linked by barbed wire into streets around the border of West Berlin. Within a day the 87-mile border was encircled by a wire fence and patrolled by guards with dogs. Eventually the 3.6 metre fence was replaced by a wall made from two million tonnes of concrete.

NATO governments were taken by surprise. In October there was a confrontation at Checkpoint Charlie (a major crossing point between East and West Berlin); ten American tanks directly faced 33 Soviet tanks in a tense 16-hour standoff. Behind the scenes, the US president spoke privately with Khrushchev and the first Soviet tank started up its engine and withdrew five yards. War had been avoided – just. In 1963, President Kennedy made a major speech at the wall, declaring to crowds of West Berliners: 'Ich bin ein Berliner' – I am a Berliner.

Between 1961 and 1989, the Berlin Wall divided the city and Germany; it became a symbol of the differences between communist and capitalist countries. Thousands of East Germans tried to escape across the wall; over a hundred died in the attempt. Eighteen-year-old Peter Fechter was shot in August 1962 and left to bleed to death in

no-man's-land. People escaped through tunnels and two families crossed the wall in a hot air balloon sewn together from curtains and sheets. Guards were ordered to shoot on sight anyone attempting to escape, even women and children.

Germans knocking down the Berlin Wall, 1989

By October 1989, the East German government was threatened by crowds of 300,000 East Germans demonstrating in the cities of Leipzig and Dresden, demanding an end to communist rule. The new East German leader, Egon Krenz, rang the Soviet leader, Mikhail Gorbachev, for advice. Unlike on previous occasions, the Soviets told the East German government not to use force, that Soviet soldiers would stay in their barracks, and that the East Germans should open the border. On 9 November, thousands of people were allowed to surge freely across the wall. With hammers and chisels, joyful Germans chipped away at it; within a year, the wall was gone and East and West Germany were reunited.

Now it's your turn

Plan and complete a museum display showing what the Berlin Wall reveals about the Cold War, East German leaders and their people, and change in the Soviet Union between 1961 and 1989.

Check your progress

I can decide what the story of the Berlin Wall reveals.
I can plan a museum display about the Berlin Wall.
I can complete my display.

Did Mikhail Gorbachev really end the Cold War?

Objectives

By the end of this lesson you will be able to:

- select evidence that supports a particular historical interpretation of Mikhail Gorbachev's role in ending the Cold War

Reagan (left) and Gorbachev (right)

In 1985 Mikhail Gorbachev became leader of the Soviet Union. He was a firm communist but knew that his country was lagging behind the rest of the world and could no longer afford the expense of the Cold War. But what could he do about this?

Getting you thinking

Look at the photograph. It shows Soviet leader Mikhail Gorbachev on the right and US President Ronald Reagan on the left in the 1980s.

- Which leader do you notice the most? Why is this?
- From the photograph, which leader might appear to have the most energy? Gorbachev was in his 50s and Reagan in his 70s.

Gorbachev realised things needed to change. He introduced 'perestroika' (restructuring) so that the Soviet government would no longer control all the economy and industry; with 'glasnost' (openness), it became easier to speak out without fear of arrest. Gorbachev negotiated with the US to reduce nuclear and other weapons. He allowed Eastern Europe to end communist rule in 1989; it was Gorbachev who advised the East German leaders to allow people to cross the Berlin Wall freely. Some historians claim that this marked the real end to the Cold War.

Gorbachev was awarded the Nobel Peace Prize in 1990 but his reforms failed in the Soviet Union itself. In 1991 it split up into many separate states and Gorbachev resigned as president. But did Gorbachev *really* end the Cold War singlehandedly?

American historian Joseph Nye claims it would have ended anyway. He says that the Soviet economy was so old-fashioned compared to NATO countries that 'the Soviet Union could not keep up. For instance, when Gorbachev came to power in 1985,

there were 50,000 personal computers in the Soviet Union; in the United States there were 30 million. Four years later there were about 400,000 personal computers in the Soviet Union and 40 million in the United States.' Whoever had become Soviet leader would have been forced to end the Cold War.

Other historians claim that the Cold War could not have been ended without the collaboration of Ronald Reagan. Reagan himself said when he visited the Soviet Union, 'Mr Gorbachev deserves most of the credit as the leader of the country.' However, after Reagan died, Gorbachev said of him that the US president's successes were 'to stop the nuclear race, start scrapping nuclear weapons and arrange normal relations between our countries'. According to historian David Greenberg 'Negotiations, not missile defence (SDI) or warlike speechmaking, marked Reagan's real contribution to ending the Cold War.'

Now it's your turn

You are a researcher to the Gorbachev Foundation in Russia today. It is a charity with a website promoting the reputation of Mikhail Gorbachev as a great leader.
1   Under a plus column list any quotes and information from these pages that you could use on the website to prove that Gorbachev really ended the Cold War. Under a minus column list any quotes and information you would leave out.
2   What information or quotes would you choose to use about Ronald Reagan's role in ending the Cold War? Remember that it is Gorbachev you are keen to show in the best light.

Check your progress

I can select some evidence in support of Gorbachev.
I can select evidence I wish to leave out, that does not support Gorbachev.
I can select evidence about Reagan seen from Gorbachev's viewpoint.

When did the Soviet Union feel most threatened by the USA from 1946 to 1983?
Part 1

During the Cold War it was difficult for Westerners to tell what Soviet leaders were really thinking or feeling, but from the archives we now know much more.

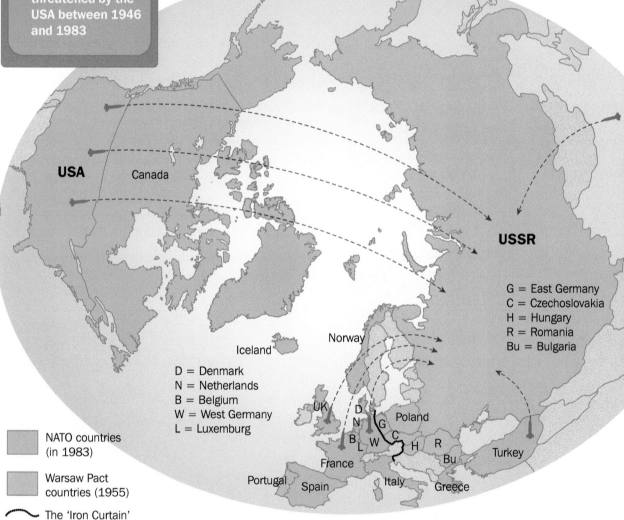

USA

Canada

USSR

G = East Germany
C = Czechoslovakia
H = Hungary
R = Romania
Bu = Bulgaria

Norway

Iceland

D = Denmark
N = Netherlands
B = Belgium
W = West Germany
L = Luxemburg

UK

D
N
B
L
W
G
C
H
R
Bu

Poland

Turkey

France

Portugal   Spain   Italy   Greece

NATO countries (in 1983)

Warsaw Pact countries (1955)

The 'Iron Curtain'

Study the map. What does it show?
- What does the map suggest about how the Soviet Union saw itself, and its relations with other world powers?

- What similarities and differences can you spot between this world map and the map on page 134?
- What has happened to NATO since 1950?

As communists, Soviet leaders believed that capitalist countries like the USA would one day collapse and that all of them would eventually be ruled by communists. But that didn't stop them being privately threatened by their enemies in NATO.

What happened

1945–1949

Communist supporters took over the Eastern European countries that were occupied by Soviet troops after World War Two. Soviet leader Josef Stalin rejected the offer of economic help for all European countries from the USA in 1948. He claimed it was a plot to undermine communism. In 1949 Stalin condemned the formation of NATO as an act of aggression and the Soviets exploded their own atomic bomb.

1950–1960

In 1950 Stalin let his ally North Korea invade America's ally South Korea. The US and its allies fought back in a war that lasted three years. In 1953 Stalin died and new Soviet leader Nikita Khrushchev improved relations with the US. In 1957 the Soviet Union launched the first satellite, Sputnik, into space. From 1956 relations with the US became difficult again when the Soviet Union invaded its ally, Hungary, to stop the country's leaders from giving more freedom to their people. Khrushchev boasted that the Soviet Union was building more and more nuclear missiles and catching up with America.

1960–1964

Khrushchev put more pressure on the US. In 1961 the two sides nearly went to war over Berlin, then Khrushchev decided to send nuclear missiles to its ally Cuba, just 180 km from the American coast. The two sides narrowly avoided nuclear war when Khruschev agreed to withdraw the missiles at the last minute. In 1964, Leonid Brezhnev replaced Khrushchev.

What soviet leaders secretly felt and thought

1945–1949

Stalin was always suspicious of the USA. He partly took over Eastern European countries so that America and its allies could not invade the Soviet Union easily. Stalin felt confident once he had the atomic bomb, as he was now America's equal.

1950–1960

Stalin was shocked when America and its allies stepped in to defend South Korea. He had not thought that they would bother and it got him worried. From 1953, new leader Nikita Khrushchev was less suspicious. However he was angered when America criticised the Soviet invasion of Hungary. Although Khrushchev was proud of Sputnik, he knew that the US had far more missiles and worried that the Soviet Union was falling behind.

1960–1964

Khrushchev thought he could pressure the young and inexperienced President Kennedy. He was shocked and appalled by how close America and the Soviet Union had come to nuclear war over Cuba. Khrushchev was relieved that he agreed a secret deal with Kennedy; the Soviet Union would withdraw its missiles from Cuba in exchange for America withdrawing its missiles from Turkey and promising not to invade Cuba. However other Soviet leaders felt the Soviet Union had been humiliated; that is why they sacked Khrushchev in 1964.

What happened

What Soviet leaders secretly felt and thought

1964–1968

The new Soviet leader, Leonid Brezhnev supported the North Vietnamese communist guerillas who were trying to take over South Vietnam. From 1965, the Vietnam War helped to pin down thousands of American troops.

In 1968 the leaders of Czechoslovakia, like Hungary in 1956, tried to give more freedom to their people. Soviet forces invaded and occupied the country. The US strongly criticised the Soviet Union.

1964–1968

Supporting North Vietnamese communist guerillas against American soldiers in South Vietnam was a way of keeping the Americans tied down in a war they could not win. It reduced the risk of a direct nuclear war between the US and the Soviet Union.

1968–1976

Relations with the USA worsened, especially in 1971 when US President Nixon visited communist China (then an enemy of the Soviet Union). However, in 1973, the USA and the Soviet Union signed SALT I, an agreement to limit nuclear weapons. Also the US pulled out of Vietnam. A period of 'détente' – understanding – led to a 'thaw' in the Cold War. In 1975, the Soviet Union signed the Helsinki Agreement with other countries, which said that it would respect human rights.

1968–1976

The Soviet leaders were very worried by Nixon's visit to China. It helped to persuade them to agree to SALT I. They saw the end of the Vietnam War as a victory for communism. Brezhnev never took the Helsinki Agreement seriously – to him it was just a piece of paper.

What happened

What soviet leaders secretly felt and thought

1976–1981

The Soviet Union was annoyed when the USA criticised it for not sticking to the Helsinki Agreement. In 1978 the Soviet government introduced new mobile SS-20 missiles into Eastern Europe. The Americans retaliated by putting cruise missiles in Western Europe. In 1979 the Soviet Union invaded Afghanistan. The US shelved a SALT II Treaty and increased defence spending.

1976–1981

The Soviet leaders were strongly divided about invading Afghanistan. By this time Brezhnev was very ill and was possibly drunk when the decision to invade was made.

1981–1983

In 1981 US President Ronald Reagan increased defence spending by 50 per cent in his first term. He made it clear that he wanted to roll back communism. In 1982, Brezhnev died and Yuri Andropov became Soviet leader. In 1983 Reagan called the Soviet Union 'an evil empire' and proposed building a satellite defence system that could shoot down Soviet missiles from space. In November 1983 Andropov nearly launched a nuclear attack on NATO when he thought that NATO military exercises were really preparations for an attack on the Warsaw Pact. It was the worst crisis since Cuba in 1962.

1981–1983

The Soviet leaders were very worried about Reagan. They knew that the Soviet Union was lagging far behind the wealth of non-communist countries. If Reagan set up a system of satellites to shoot down Soviet missiles, the Soviet Union could never afford to do the same. The Soviet leaders genuinely thought that Reagan meant to launch a nuclear attack against the Warsaw Pact.

Now it's your turn

1 Plot a graph with the years 1946 to 1983 along the bottom. Down the side at the bottom put 'not threatened at all', in the middle 'quite threatened' and at the top 'very threatened'. Plot events or factors you think made the Soviets more or less threatened by America.
2 When did the Soviet Union feel most threatened?
3 Why was this?

Check your progress

I can plot a graph showing how much the Soviet Union felt threatened by the USA.
I can decide when it felt most threatened.
I can suggest why this was.

Why did the USA oppose Iran's Islamic Revolution?

The Soviet Union was not the only threat to the United States during the Cold War. In 1979, it faced a dangerous revolution in Iran, a country that supplied it with vital energy in the form of oil.

Getting you thinking

Look at the picture.

- What impression do you get of this man's character from this photograph?

The picture shows the leader of Iran's Islamic Revolution, Ayatollah Khomeini. Khomeini was a Muslim cleric (holy man) from Iran who was living in exile in Paris. This was because he was a powerful enemy of Iran's Shah (emperor). Iran was and is a very traditional Muslim country. Iran is rich in oil and the Shah used this wealth to try and modernise the country. Rich people and many middle-class people were able to follow foreign trends, such as women going out in public with no head covering, or drinking alcohol. The Shah even changed the traditional Muslim calendar for a new imperial one. Religious leaders like Khomeini, who commanded the loyalty of many Iranians, denounced the Shah. However the Shah kept tight control through his ruthless secret police (Savak).

Ayatollah Khomeini

During and after the Cold War, although American governments always claimed to support freedom and democracy, they sometimes backed governments which did not believe in either. An American president once said of a dictator who was an ally: 'he may be a son of a bitch, but he's our son of a bitch.' The Shah was such an ally. Although he was a dictator, the US supported him because:

- the Shah was strongly anti-communist, and Savak kept communists under strict control
- Iran's oil was a vital supply of energy for the US and its allies
- Iran's powerful armed forces deterred the Soviet Union or anti-American governments like Iraq from trying to seize control of its oilfields or those of Arab counties nearby

In 1979 the Shah was overthrown. Ayatollah Khomeini returned from exile and set up an Islamic republic. He became supreme leader and his supporters controlled the country strictly; enemies of the revolution could be shot. Traditional Muslim customs and laws were imposed; alcohol was banned and the streets were patrolled by Revolutionary Guards who might arrest women with no head coverings or unmarried couples holding hands in public. Khomeini blamed the United States for keeping the Shah in power, and called it the 'Great Satan'. On 4 November 1979, Iranian students held 66 Americans hostage in the US embassy. A rescue mission in April 1980 was bungled when a helicopter and an aircraft collided, killing eight American servicemen.

Khomeini threatened to spread his anti-American Islamic revolution to other Muslim countries. His government also denounced America's ally, Israel (the Jewish state), because it claimed that Israelis had driven Muslim Palestinians from their homeland in 1948 and continued to treat them badly. Communism was no longer the only enemy of the United States. In 2010 Khomeini's supporters still controlled Iran. The US accused them of trying to develop nuclear weapons.

Now it's your turn

1 List causes that explain why the US opposed Iran's Islamic revolution.
2 Write down the headings: Political causes; Social causes; Economic causes; Religious causes. Group the reasons that you listed for question 1 under each of these headings.
3 Which do you think were the most important causes and why?

Check your progress

I can list causes of US opposition to Iran's Islamic revolution.

I can organise causes under different headings.

I can choose which causes I think were most important and explain the reasons for my choices.

Why did Osama bin Laden turn against America?

Osama bin Laden was born in Saudi Arabia in 1957, the son of a rich businessman. Brought up as a strict Muslim, he did not stand out at school. Yet bin Laden became one of America's most hated and feared enemies.

FBI TEN MOST WANTED FUGITIVE

MURDER OF U.S. NATIONALS OUTSIDE THE UNITED STATES;
CONSPIRACY TO MURDER U.S. NATIONALS OUTSIDE THE UNITED STATES;
ATTACK ON A FEDERAL FACILITY RESULTING IN DEATH

USAMA BIN LADEN

Date of Photograph Unknown

Aliases: Usama Bin Muhammad Bin Ladin, Shaykh Usama Bin Ladin, the Prince, the Emir, Abu Abdallah, Mujahid Shaykh, Hajj, the Director

DESCRIPTION

Date of Birth:	1957	Hair:	Brown
Place of Birth:	Saudi Arabia	Eyes:	Brown
Height:	6' 4" to 6' 6"	Complexion:	Olive
Weight:	Approximately 160 pounds	Sex:	Male
Build:	Thin	Nationality:	Saudi Arabian
Occupation(s):	Unknown		
Remarks:	He is the leader of a terrorist organization known as Al-Qaeda "The Base." He walks with a cane.		

CAUTION

USAMA BIN LADEN IS WANTED IN CONNECTION WITH THE AUGUST 7, 1998, BOMBINGS OF THE UNITED STATES EMBASSIES IN DAR ES SALAAM, TANZANIA AND NAIROBI, KENYA. THESE ATTACKS KILLED OVER 200 PEOPLE.

CONSIDERED ARMED AND EXTREMELY DANGEROUS

IF YOU HAVE ANY INFORMATION CONCERNING THIS PERSON, PLEASE CONTACT YOUR LOCAL FBI OFFICE OR THE NEAREST U.S. EMBASSY OR CONSULATE.

REWARD

The United States Government is offering a reward of up to $5 million for information leading directly to the apprehension or conviction of Usama Bin Laden.

FBI 'wanted' poster of Osama bin Laden, 1999

Getting you thinking

Study the picture.

- What is bin Laden accused of in this American poster from 1999?
- What indicates the importance that the American FBI (Federal Bureau of Investigation) attached to catching him?

So how did an ordinary Muslim boy ever get to be on this poster? The answer is not simple. Like anybody, bin Laden did not set out to become a terrorist, but his life was like a journey, where important twists and turns, sometimes beyond his control, shaped him. Osama's father died when he was only 13 and he married quite young, at 17. He went to university in Saudi Arabia; however, he was much more interested in Islam than in his studies. He inherited money from his father. Bin Laden was influenced by a group of Saudis who were ready to criticise their country's government for not being strict enough Muslims. He learnt to despise both the godless communists of the Soviet Union and the Americans, whom he distrusted as mostly Christians who also supported Israel, the Jewish state established in 1948.

To some Saudis it was unacceptable that their government could be an ally of America, when Jews who had settled in Israel were accused of stealing Arab land and persecuting Muslim Palestinians. It also seemed a disgrace that Jerusalem, Islam's third holiest city, should be ruled by Israel. The 1977 American-backed peace agreement between Israel and its old enemy Egypt seemed a betrayal. The anti-American Islamic Revolution in Iran in 1979 (see pages 150–151) also showed the young Osama what Muslim power could do. The Soviet invasion of Muslim Afghanistan, also in 1979 (see page 138), seemed a god-given opportunity for Muslims who were serious about fighting for their faith to go there and prove themselves. If they died fighting in this *jihad* they would become martyrs, going straight to heaven.

Many Saudis volunteered to fight in Afghanistan. In 1984 bin Laden moved to Peshawar in Pakistan, on the border with Afghanistan, where he organised Muslims from abroad, mostly from Arab countries, who were willing to fight as *jihadis* against the Soviets. The Saudi government and the Americans approved at the time. This did not mean that bin Laden now liked the Americans; it just happened that the Soviets were then the greater enemy.

By 1988 bin Laden had established Al-Qaeda, a network of *jihadis* that outlasted Soviet defeat in 1989. When the Iraqi leader Saddam Hussein invaded Kuwait in 1990, bin Laden offered the Saudi government Al-Qaeda fighters to defend his homeland. To his utter disgust, they turned him down and instead trusted the Americans and their allies to defeat Saddam. Even worse, American troops were based on the sacred soil of Saudi Arabia itself. It was Americans that were to be the target of Al-Qaeda's new *jihad*.

Now it's your turn

Sketch bin Laden's life from 1957 to 1990 like a road with important dates marked on it. Make it twist or turn sharply where you decide something important happened.

Check your progress

I can sketch a road showing bin Laden's life.
I can mark key dates on the sketch.
I can draw a sketch that shows which dates are most important.

Jihadi: active Muslim supporter of holy war
Jihad: holy war

Objectives

By the end of this lesson you will be able to:

- identify historical problems and then suggest and evaluate possible solutions

Osama bin Laden finally turned decisively against the United States in 1990. He fled first to Sudan and then to Afghanistan where some very extreme *jihadi* fighters called the Taliban seized power in 1996. But how do bin Laden and his fellow veterans of the *jihad* against the Soviet occupation of Afghanistan see the rest of the world?

Getting you thinking

7 2003 onwards: US and British forces invade and occupy Iraq to overthrow dictator Saddam Hussein. Al-Qaeda and other jihadis kill thousands of people including fellow Muslims through terror attacks

1 1998: Al-Qaeda explosion demolishes US embassy in Nairobi, killing 213 people, mostly non-Americans

8 2002 onwards: American forces help to overthrow the Taliban government for sheltering Al-Qaeda. American and allied troops, including British soldiers, die in attacks by Taliban rebels

2 1998: Al-Qaeda attack on US embassy in Dar es Salaam killing 11 people

3 2000: Al-Qaeda attack on US navy ship Cole, killing 17

9 At various times Israelis have been killed by Palestinian rocket attacks and suicide bombers. At other times this has developed into full-scale war. Foreign jihadis have volunteered to fight with certain Palestinian groups

4 1993: Jihadi explosion in World Trade Centre, New York, killing six

5 2001: Al-Qaeda hijack four passenger planes and crash some into the twin towers of the World Trade Centre in New York. Nearly 3,000 people die

10 October 2002: Chechen terrorists seized a Moscow theatre, which was stormed by Russian troops, killing over 100 people

6 1998: America fires cruise missiles at an Al-Qaeda training camp

11 September 2004: Over 300 people killed, including many school children when Chechen terrorists seize a school, which is stormed by Russian troops

12 First Chechen War 1994–96: Foreign jihadis volunteer to fight with Muslim Chechen rebels to win independence from Russia

13 Second Chechen War 1999–2000: Foreign jihadis lead an invasion of Russian territory, which gives Russia the excuse to re-conquer Chechnya

United States

Study the map.

- How many wars can you count?
- How many countries have suffered terror attacks?

Jihadis like bin Laden:

- are prepared to fight anywhere in the world to help fellow Muslims attack their enemies
- believe in a very strict worldwide Muslim government, not democracy
- are prepared to die for their cause and, if necessary, kill innocent people including fellow Muslims

Now it's your turn

1 List problems you can think of in trying to stop terror attacks by jihadis and their supporters.
2 For each problem suggest a solution.
3 How many new problems might your solutions create?

Check your progress

I can list problems in trying to stop terror attacks.
I can suggest solutions to these problems.
I can suggest new problems that my suggested solutions might create.

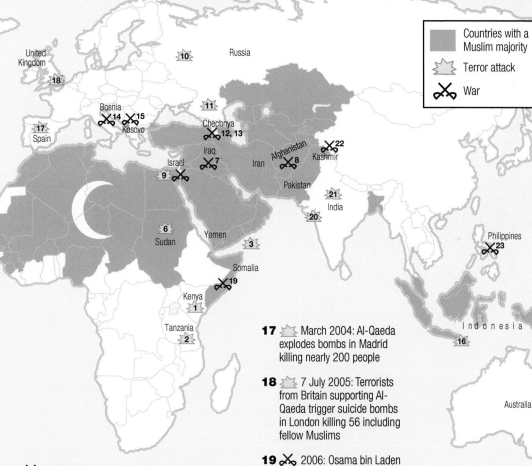

17 March 2004: Al-Qaeda explodes bombs in Madrid killing nearly 200 people

18 7 July 2005: Terrorists from Britain supporting Al-Qaeda trigger suicide bombs in London killing 56 including fellow Muslims

19 2006: Osama bin Laden calls on foreign jihadis to help some Somali groups

14 1992–95: Foreign jihadis fight alongside Bosnian Muslims against their enemies

15 1997–99: Some foreign jihadis volunteer to help Muslim Albanians in Kosovo rebel against Serbia

16 October 2002: A group linked to Al-Qaeda explodes a bomb in Bali killing over 200 people, including many tourists from America's ally, Australia. A further bombing in 2005 kills 20

20 November 2008: Kashmiri terrorists based in Pakistan attack Mumbai, killing over 100 people

21 December 2001: Kashmiri terrorists attack the Indian parliament in New Dehli

22 Over many years Kashmiri Muslim rebels have fought India for independence

23 Over many years Muslim rebels have fought for independence for their part of the Phillipines

What did 9/11 reveal about the United States?

Objectives

By the end of this lesson you will be able to:

- suggest what a particular event reveals about its historical significance

The last time a battle was fought in mainland America was during the Civil War of the 1860s. American soldiers have fought in wars all over the world but American cities were never bombed and civilian life went on largely untouched. Food was never rationed, children were never evacuated, no time was spent huddling in air raid shelters, foreign troops never occupied the mainland. When the threat of total nuclear destruction lifted at the end of the Cold War, it seemed that the world's remaining superpower was even more invulnerable to attack on its own soil than ever before.

Second aeroplane crashing into the twin towers on September 11, 2001

Getting you thinking

Look at the picture.

- Why might some Americans have assumed at first that these plane crashes were an accident?
- Do you find the photograph shocking or not? Why is this?

On 11 September 2001, thousands of people were going about their daily business in the twin towers of the World Trade Centre in New York. Suddenly, out of a clear blue sky, an airliner crashed into one of the towers, followed later by a second plane into the other tower. All over the world viewers watched live coverage as trapped individuals jumped to their deaths from upper floors and as the towers subsequently collapsed. 'Windows were shattered,' said one eyewitness, 'people were screaming and diving for cover … [they] walked around like ghosts, covered in dirt, weeping and wandering dazed.' Another hijacked airliner smashed into *the Pentagon* in Washington while a fourth crash-landed in a field when passengers and crew tried to overpower the terrorists. Nearly 3,000 people died that day, including 19 of Al-Qaeda's hijackers. America and the world were profoundly shocked.

Police officers and rescue workers from across the country took leave of absence to help with the recovery of bodies. Offers to donate blood soared and charities raised money quickly for bereaved families. Politicians sang 'God bless America' on the steps of the *Capitol*. All flights in North America were grounded. Hate crimes and harassment of anyone with a 'middle eastern appearance' grew; mosques were attacked and Sikhs, mistaken for Muslims because of their turbans, were also victimised. A Hindu temple mistaken for a mosque was firebombed. Many American Muslims condemned the attacks. 'I don't want to see this religion (Islam) used … to justify mass murder sprees,' complained New York lawyer Asama Khan, who formed the group Muslims Against Terrorism.

Senator John McCain claimed 'everybody is talking about a second Pearl Harbour' (see page 103). The public initially rallied around President Bush who passed new laws creating a department of Homeland Security and giving government agents more powers to tap telephones etc. He launched a 'War on Terror', which overthrew the Taliban government in Afghanistan in 2002 for sheltering Al-Qaeda (see pages 154–155). In 2003 an American led coalition invaded and occupied Iraq, partly on the (mistaken) grounds that its dictator, Saddam Hussein, was linked to Al-Qaeda (see pages 154–155). Some Americans insist that the incident, which has become known as 9/11, was actually a plot by their own government to justify foreign conquest and increased powers.

Now it's your turn

1 List what you think 9/11 reveals about America as a country on a mind map.
2 Add supporting detail to each point on your mind map.
3 Use a range of colours to highlight which points you think are the most and least important in what they reveal about the country.

Check your progress

⭐ I can list points on a mind map.
⭐⭐ I can add supporting detail.
⭐⭐⭐ I can identify the most important and the least important points.

Pentagon: USA military headquarters
Capitol: where US Congress meets in Washington

How successful has foreign intervention been in Afghanistan since 1838?

Since 2006, the bodies of over 100 British soldiers have been returned from Afghanistan. But why are British and other troops there? How can we measure the success of foreign intervention in Afghanistan?

Getting you thinking

Look at the photograph. It shows a war memorial in Dorset.

- Does it look like a 20th century design?
- Would it surprise you to know that it commemorates British soldiers killed on the Afghan border during Queen Victoria's reign?

As we have seen (see map of Afghanistan on page 138) Afghanistan is very difficult for any government to control. The table opposite describes foreign intervention since 1838.

War memorial in Dorchester

Now it's your turn

1 How do you think we should decide if foreign intervention in Afghanistan has been successful since 1838?
2 On a line with one end marked successful and the other unsuccessful, plot where you judge each of these interventions listed in the table should be placed.

Reprisals: military action in response to an enemy's attacks

Date	Intervention	Results
1838–1842	**First Anglo-Afghan War:** British troops invaded Afghanistan to block Russian influence. There were too few soldiers to occupy the country, and they had to retreat to British India. They were massacred on the way.	The British launched military *reprisals* for their defeat but did not attempt to re-occupy Afghanistan. The Russian Empire continued to expand southwards towards Afghanistan and British India.
1878–1880	**Second Anglo-Afghan War:** The British occupied Afghanistan for two years, crushing any revolts and installing a pro-British ruler.	The British did not stay in Afghanistan but the Afghan ruler had to agree to let Britain control its relations with foreign governments. This helped to block Russian influence.
1914–1918	**Turkish and German influence:** At the outbreak of World War One, the Ottoman Empire tried to persuade the Afghan ruler to join its jihad against Britain. Germany encouraged the Afghans to recover their independence.	The Afghan ruler was not tempted to fight against Britain but it made him want to recover his independence. When the British Indian Army appeared exhausted at the end of World War One, he saw his chance to change things.
1919	**Third Anglo-Afghan War:** Afghan troops invaded British India but were defeated. Royal Air Force planes bombed Kabul.	The Afghan ruler won back complete control of his foreign policy.
1978–1989	**Soviet occupation:** In 1978 Afghan communists seized power in Kabul. In 1979 Soviet forces invaded and occupied Afghanistan. The USA and other countries armed the Mujahadeen, a group of Afghan Muslim rebels.	The Soviets were forced to withdraw defeated in 1989. The communist government was overthrown in 1992 but a civil war between the *Mujahadeen* followed. The *Taliban* seized power in 1996 giving protection to former jihadi Osama bin laden and Al-Qaeda.
2002 onwards	**US-led coalition invasion and occupation:** The US supported some Afghans in overthrowing the *Taliban* government. A Taliban rebellion threatened to return them to power and make the country a base to spread Al-Qaeda terror worldwide. NATO helped keep elected president Hamid Karzai in power by occupying Afghanistan, fighting the Taliban and rebuilding the country.	American and British public opinion has grown weary of the Afghan war. NATO leaders are hoping Afghan police and soldiers will be able to take over from their troops in resisting the Taliban. However, a Taliban spokesman said in 2009, 'You have the watch, we have the time'.

Check your progress

I can decide what successful means.
I can plot interventions on the line.
I can justify my choices with reference to evidence.

Mujahadeen: Muslim rebel fighters
Taliban: radical Islamic group

Was the invasion of Iraq a 'recruiting sergeant' for Al-Qaeda?

On 20 March 2003, a coalition of forces led by the USA began the invasion of Iraq. President Bush claimed that the aim of the war was to 'disarm Iraq of weapons of mass destruction (WMD), to end Saddam Hussein's support for terrorism and to free the Iraqi people'. The Iraqi regime collapsed quickly and the main military campaign was over by 1 May that year. But would the coalition be able to win the hearts and minds of ordinary Iraqis?

Getting you thinking

Look at the photograph. It shows US marines spreading an American flag across the face of a statue of Saddam Hussein during the fall of Baghdad in 2003.

- Whose flag might you have expected the marines to put on the statue?
- What might Iraqis watching this event have made of this scene?

The American military had planned the invasion well but plans for the occupation were poor. Inexperienced Americans sometimes found themselves in charge of whole Iraqi ministries. The Iraqi army was disbanded, but there were too few coalition soldiers to keep law and order; looting and corruption became major problems. The coalition was not helped by the fact that two of Bush's claims for going to war were discredited; no WMD were ever found, and it was proved that there had never been any cooperation between Saddam and terrorists like Al-Qaeda.

In the absence of strong central government, and occupied by unpopular foreign troops, Iraqi groups competed for power. The Kurds in the north hoped for self-government. The majority Shia Muslims, *persecuted* by Saddam, turned for protection to religious *militia* leaders. Some of the Sunni Muslim minority, deprived of the power they had enjoyed under Saddam, joined Al-Qaeda.

During Saddam's rule Al-Qaeda had not operated in Iraq, but the power vacuum created by the invasion allowed them in. Al-Qaeda aimed to force the withdrawal of foreign troops by making Iraq ungovernable. Any Iraqi who *collaborated* was targeted for assassination. For example, 49 unarmed recruits for the new Iraqi National Guard

Persecute: victimise, harass or treat unfairly because of religion or ethnic origins
Militia: unfficial, private army made up of civilians

were captured and massacred. Some foreign hostages were kidnapped, beheaded with knives, and films of the murders posted on the internet. To increase conflict between Sunni and Shia Muslims, *suicide bombers* targeted Shia civilians attending worship, indiscriminately killing hundreds of men, women and children. This had the desired effect of provoking attacks on innocent Sunnis by Shia militia.

The loss of life was of no concern to Al-Qaeda. Parts of the country were in chaos. From 2007 American generals put more troops on the streets, and recruited thousands of former Iraqi rebels to resist the foreign led Al-Qaeda terrorists. Law and order improved; more power was given to the elected government, while Al-Qaeda seemed to lose support and influence. In 2009 British forces withdrew from Iraq and the US hoped to be able to do the same eventually. However, suicide bombings continued in Iraq in 2010.

US marines putting an American flag over the face of Saddam Hussein's statue during the fall of Baghdad

Now it's your turn

1 What did the Americans and their allies do or fail to do in Iraq that might have attracted some Iraqis to support Al-Qaeda?
2 What advice might you have given President Bush in 2002 knowing what we know has happened in Iraq since then?

Check your progress

I can identify at least one thing that the Americans did or failed to do.

I can identify several things that the Americans did or failed to do.

I can use recent events in Iraq to advise as if it were 2002.

Collaborated: *worked with the coalition*
Suicide bomber: *someone prepared to kill themselves to injure others*

China under Mao Zedong

Objectives

By the end of this lesson you will be able to:

- analyse the causes of division between two states

Communists seized power in China in 1949, giving Joseph Stalin's Soviet Union a powerful new ally. Yet by the early 1960s Soviet leader Nikita Khrushchev was not on speaking terms with Chinese leader Mao Zedong. Despite this, the USA regarded Red China as a dangerous enemy. Why was this?

Getting you thinking

Look at this Chinese communist poster from the 1960s.
- What colour stands out most from this poster?
- What do you notice most prominently in the background?

It shows a muscular, young Chinese worker striding boldly across the poster. The original caption with the poster read 'Let philosophy (ways of thinking) become a weapon of the people!' He is carried forward on a sea of red communist banners, urged onwards by the Chinese people

Chinese communist poster from the 1960s

Collective farms: *state owned but run by the peasants*
Cultural Revolution: *attempt to completely change public opinion and behaviour*

below him. In his hand he clasps the 'Little Red Book' containing quotations from Mao Zedong and which the Communist Party encourages him to apply completely in everyday life. Behind, a mushroom cloud caused by an atomic bomb, surges into the sky (China carried out its first nuclear test in 1964).

Why might this type of art have worried many Americans? The first image was evidence that communist China was proud of its nuclear programme and unafraid to use it. Such weapons could be directed against the United States as well as the Soviet Union, making the world a more dangerous place. Mao's attitude towards a possible nuclear war was ruthless. Huge underground bunkers were constructed but he always said that even after a nuclear attack the Chinese would quickly replace those killed with millions of new babies.

Communist badges with Mao's portrait

The image represents a way of life and political system that was totally at odds with American capitalism and personal freedoms. Political power lay solely in the hands of the Communist Party. The Little Red Book claimed: 'The Chinese Communist Party is the core leadership of the whole Chinese people.' Freedom of speech was virtually impossible. The peasants worked on *collective farms* and personal profit was banned.

In 1966, to consolidate his grip over the Communist Party, Mao launched a *Cultural Revolution*, urging the youthful Red Guards to criticise their communist elders. Any activity labelled bourgeois or middle class could be attacked or banned, traditional cultural symbols such as temples were smashed, older people and experienced party officials could be denounced, beaten up, imprisoned or killed. Students and *intellectuals* were often *exiled* to work on the land with the peasants for years at a time. The Red Guards used to chant: 'Every letter in Chairman Mao's words is gold and every sentence is truth. Fish cannot live without water and without Mao Zedong's thought how can people make revolution?' Perhaps a million people died as a result of the Cultural Revolution. The Chinese might not have had as many nuclear weapons or as much power as the Soviets in the 1960s but Mao was more ruthless and fanatical with a vast population under his control.

Now it's your turn

Complete an outline sketch of the figures and features in the poster. Label these and add supporting notes for what they tell us about communist China in the 1960s. Write a sentence summarising the most important things it tells us.

Check your progress

I can draw the sketch.
I can label and add supporting notes to the sketch.
I can summarise the key arguments in a sentence.

Intellectual: academic, person who works with their mind, thinker
Exiled: forced to move away from home and friends

What did the Beijing Olympics of 2008 reveal about China?

Objectives

By the end of this lesson you will be able to:

- assess the historical significance of a particular event

In 2008 an estimated 4.7 billion people watched the Olympic Games in Beijing, which cost £20 billion to stage. On an official Chinese website one Beijing resident commented: 'It was like a huge international party. I was very proud of my country hosting the whole world'. According to Professor Hu Angang, quoted on the same website, 'After 30 years of development, China, with a population of 1.3 billion, has totally become a part of the world…'

Getting you thinking

Look at the picture of the main Olympic stadium.

- Can you see why it was called the Bird's Nest Stadium?
- Can you see evidence of its £250 million cost?

The Chinese Communist Party was eager to show how much China has achieved since the end of Mao's Cultural Revolution through the staging of the games. In 1976 the state-controlled economy was in

Bird's Nest Stadium, Beijing

chaos, people dressed in identical Mao suits, the main form of transport was the bicycle and China was largely cut off from the outside world.

The official Chinese Olympic website claims:

China's current spell of fast development dates from 1978, when the whole country had just emerged from the mania of the 10 year Cultural Revolution … The past three decades have seen an average growth rate of almost 10 per cent a year, making China the fourth largest economy … With economic power, China had the money for hosting the games.

Individuals were encouraged to set up businesses and make money, people adopted western dress and business suits, modern skyscrapers sprang up in the major cities, streets became choked with cars and pollution. China, like Britain before it, became the workshop of the world, exporting its cheaply made goods everywhere.

Yet despite the huge economic changes, political power still lay with the Chinese Communist Party. It violently *suppressed* a student movement demanding democratic *reform* in 1989. It has even succeeded in forcing internet companies to censor their content.

In the run up to the Olympic Games, 1.5 million Chinese people were forcibly rehoused to make way for development. Human Rights group Amnesty International claimed: 'In the run up to the Olympic Games, the Chinese authorities have locked up, put under house arrest and forcibly removed individuals they believe threaten the image of "stability" and "harmony" they want to present to the world.' Any foreigners attempting protests, for example demanding independence for Tibet, were swiftly bundled out of the country. China has not only used its economic power to stage sporting events. Although it cannot as yet match the military spending of the United States, China increased its military budget by 194 per cent between 1999 and 2008, and increased its spending on nuclear weapons by 25 per cent between 2006 and 2008.

Now it's your turn

Create a poster of the 2008 Olympic Games, selecting things that the Chinese government might show off as achievements of the Games themselves, and of China's progress since 1976. The Olympic slogan was 'One World, One Dream'.
What would you choose to leave out?

Check your progress

I can create an Olympic poster from the Chinese perspective.
I can comment on what to leave out of the poster.
I can comment on the changes in China since the 1970s.

Suppressed: put down, destroy
Reform: change

What did the makers of *Invictus* choose to leave out about Nelson Mandela?

Nelson Mandela, South Africa's first black president, attended the 1995 Rugby World Cup Final in the city of Johannesburg, hoping to rally the country's divided black and white population around the largely white national rugby team, the Springboks. Mandela donned a Springboks green and orange shirt to greet the players including team captain, Francois Pienaar. The mostly white crowd of spectators roared out 'Nel-son, Nel-son'. The Springboks beat the New Zealand All Blacks 15-12.

Mandela meeting Pienaar

Freeman meeting Damon

Getting you thinking

Look at the top photograph showing Mandela greeting Pienaar in 1995 and the bottom photograph showing Hollywood actors re-enacting the same scene for a 2009 film.

- How closely does actor Morgan Freeman resemble Mandela?
- How closely does actor Matt Damon resemble Pienaar?

The filmmakers of *Invictus* (the title of a poem that inspired Mandela) had to make choices about what to put in their film about the 1995 Rugby World Cup. They left out details of Mandela's early life; so viewers do not see the young Mandela, proud of his fit boxer's body and immaculately dressed by the same tailor as South Africa's richest white millionaire. Nor does this film show his support for the violent overthrow of the government, which resulted in his imprisonment on *Robben Island*. Mandela slept on a thin straw mat in a small cell and washed in seawater for most of his 27 years there. It was this experience that transformed Mandela's views.

During the decades of South African apartheid (literally 'separate development') from 1948 to 1994, the country's black majority were deprived of their human rights including the vote, treated brutally by racist police and soldiers, and forced to live in overcrowded townships or wretched countryside. Many whites, however, lived well in fine houses, on the best land, and were served by black employees. Despite all this Mandela became convinced that forgiveness and *reconciliation* were better ways forward than violence.

In jail he learnt the Afrikaans language of the main white group, the Afrikaners. He befriended his guards and combined his natural charm with a growing knowledge of their history and passions, including rugby. Once he was released Mandela helped the last white president, F. W. de Klerk, negotiate an end to apartheid and organise free elections.

What the film shows is how prior to the World Cup Mandela worked with Pienaar to persuade blacks that the hated white rugby team could become a symbol of the new South Africa. It also suggests that Mandela worked hard to reconcile whites, thus avoiding a potential civil war and demands for a separate white state. However, critics of 'Invictus' complain that:

the film leaves out the food poisoning that affected most of the All Blacks team just two days before the final. In his 1996 biography, their coach stated that a group of Far Eastern gamblers bribed a waitress to poison the water served in their hotel, a claim backed up in 2001 by one of Mandela's bodyguards.

the film ends in 1995, giving the impression that Mandela solved all South Africa's problems. Critics point out that poor blacks are still poor, corruption and crime are common and HIV/AIDS is widespread.

Now it's your turn

1   What impression of Mandela and South Africa does *Invictus* intend to give?
2   Why might that impression have changed had the filmmakers included Mandela's early life, the food poisoning and South Africa since 1995?
3   Using additional research, design a storyboard for a film of Mandela's life.

Check your progress

I can decide what impression of Nelson Mandela and South Africa the film intends to give.

I can say how that impression would change if other incidents were included.

I can design a film storyboard showing a complete picture of Mandela's life.

Reconciliation: being prepared to be friends with former enemies

Creating historical interpretations

Sometimes the creators of historical interpretations are very careful about the information and facts they use to support their view of the past. Noticing what has been included tells you a lot about what they think was important about an event, period or person. Knowing what has been left out may tell you what they think is either unimportant or may contradict their interpretation.

Getting you thinking

This is the badge of the American aircraft carrier USS Ronald Reagan, launched in 2001 and named after former president Ronald Reagan (1981-89). Look carefully at the images on the badge and the labels that explain them.

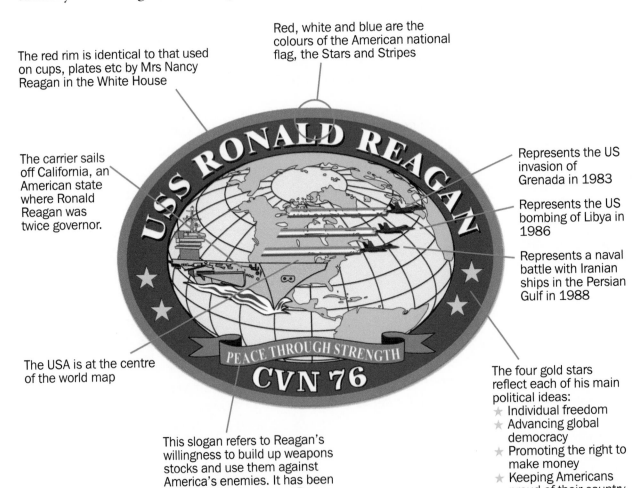

Red, white and blue are the colours of the American national flag, the Stars and Stripes

The red rim is identical to that used on cups, plates etc by Mrs Nancy Reagan in the White House

The carrier sails off California, an American state where Ronald Reagan was twice governor.

Represents the US invasion of Grenada in 1983

Represents the US bombing of Libya in 1986

Represents a naval battle with Iranian ships in the Persian Gulf in 1988

The USA is at the centre of the world map

The four gold stars reflect each of his main political ideas:
  ★ Individual freedom
  ★ Advancing global democracy
  ★ Promoting the right to make money
  ★ Keeping Americans proud of their country

This slogan refers to Reagan's willingness to build up weapons stocks and use them against America's enemies. It has been claimed that this helped Reagan win the Cold War.

What impression of Ronald Reagan and America do you get from this seal?

Why might the following have been left out?
- Reagan's backing for a brutal anti-communist military government in El Salvador (Central America)
- The secret sale of weapons to Iran to pay for weapons for anti-communist rebels in Nicaragua (Central America)

Barack Obama was elected president of the United States in 2008. Born in 1961 in Hawaii to a white, American mother and a black, Muslim father from Kenya, he went to university in California and to Harvard Law School. Obama became a Christian as an adult and worked as a community organiser in Chicago. He became senator for the state of Illinois before being elected as the country's first African-American president. At his inauguration Obama said: 'America is strong because its people come from many different backgrounds, cultures, countries and skin colours. We are a nation of Christians and Muslims, Jews and Hindus – and non-believers … America must play its role in ushering in a new era of peace … values upon which our success depends – hard work and honesty, courage and fair play, tolerance and curiosity, loyalty and patriotism…'

Now it's your turn

You have been asked to design the seal for a US warship to be named Barack Obama. As one of his supporters, design, create and label a seal for him based on what you know about him, explaining reasons for the choices you have made. You could research some of the symbols of the places he has been. Check up on his record as president. Do you think there is anything you would choose to leave out? How and why is your design for Barack Obama different from the one for Ronald Reagan?

Check your level

I can design and label my seal for USS Barack Obama with details based on his life and ideas.	I can design and label my seal. I can say why I have chosen some details and not others.	I can design and label my seal. I can say why I have chosen some details and left out others. I can explain how and why my design differs from that for Ronald Reagan. My answers show that I understand why interpretations of history like these can vary so much.

Level 5

Level 6

Level 7

5

Life in Britain in the twentieth century

Below is a photograph of Lewisham High Street, taken at the start of the 20th century. How similar is it to your local high street today?

Can you imagine what it would be like going shopping without a supermarket or frozen foods? Stores like Marks and Spencer and Sainsbury's were just starting out, but they were very different from today. Most foods came in bulk to shopkeepers. For example, tea would come in great big chests, flour in barrels and butter in big blocks. Each item needed to be weighed out separately and wrapped up for the customer. Shopping needed to be done every day.

Questions

1 How many different kinds of transport can you identify in the photograph?

2 How many different kinds of shops can you find? Would you expect to find the same kind of shops in the high street today?

3 Do you think the people in the photograph are well-off, or poor? How can you tell?

4 After looking at the photograph, what, in your opinion, has been the biggest change in the high street over the last 100 years?

A local history toolkit

History is all around us. Even the tiniest village has its own history; it is often surprisingly interesting! Let's find out some of the ways we might explore local history.

Getting you thinking

Tools for local history

1. Aerial photographs

They make an excellent starting point for exploring your neighbourhood. Pick out key features from the pictures and compare them with the area today.

2. Old maps

Ordinance Survey maps at various scales are particularly useful for showing change over the century. Try 6" to a mile maps to really look in detail at the area around you.

3. Trade directories

These are a fascinating source of detailed information about your area. They were published throughout the 20th century.

This entry describes the village and its services. It also lists all the main landowners and trades people. By using several directories over a period of time, you can trace some families in a similar way to using census material.

Kelly's trade directory, 1913

4. Old photographs

This one shows the village water pump in use. Elderly residents in the village can usually tell you where different pieces of *street furniture* were situated. The writers of this book arranged a coffee morning in the local chapel and asked residents to loan us their old photographs. Many were happy to do so.

Village water pump

5. Old newspapers

Many local newspapers have been in existence for hundreds of years, and are a great source of local history. The British Library has recently digitised its collection, so your local paper might be available online. Otherwise, visit your local library or county records office.

Street furniture: objects for public use – post boxes, benches etc
Prize money: share of the money from a captured ship

6. Census data

Censuses have been taken at ten-year intervals since 1801. At present censuses from 1901 and 1911 are available to view online, although you have to pay to download them.

A page from the Little Hale census, 1901

7. Old advertisements

Trade directories had pages of these at the back, but old newspapers are equally useful for finding the unusual and different. Imagine, for example, a world when ice was delivered by train to your door! What a great source to explain change and continuity over time.

8. Oral history

You may be lucky enough to live in a town or village that has a large number of families who have lived in the area for a long time. Ask them about the local school. The father-in-law of one of this book's authors had Italian prisoners of war working on his farm during World War Two – this was an interesting way to talk about both the war and local history.

9. Contact your local history society

One of their members might be working on your neighbourhood. Even if no one is, they will know where the relevant records are kept. They will also know lots of interesting anecdotes, like the story of the sailor who is buried in a local churchyard. Apparently, he was walking home from the Napoleonic Wars, with lots of *prize money*, and stopped for a drink in the local pub. Next morning he was found robbed and murdered on the turnpike; his murderer was never caught.

10. Visit your local library and county records office

The *archivist* will be only too happy to help, if you have a clear idea of what you want.

11. Visit your local museum

The Museum of Lincolnshire Life, for example, has a terrific collection of farm carts, machinery etc that helps to bring rural history to life. There is also a tank from World War One – built in Lincoln of course – as well as the Regimental Museum of the Lincolnshire Regiment.

Now it's your turn APP

Which of these tools do you think are the most useful for studying local history? Why?

Archivist: someone who looks after the records

What can old photographs tell us about local history?

People say 'the camera never lies'. They also say that 'a photograph is worth a thousand words'. If that is the case then we may be able to discover a great deal about Edwardian times, and plot many of the changes that have happened since then, by looking at the two photographs on the right.

Getting you thinking

As you saw in the previous lesson, old photographs can help us understand the story of our neighbourhood – if we can ask them the right questions. What questions can we ask of this old photograph? And what does having a 'modern' photograph to compare it with add to our understanding of history?

Kelly's Directory for Little Hale, 1913, lists Thomas Dickinson as the landlord of the Bowling Green public house. He was also landlord in 1905. We can use both the 1901 and 1911 census for Little Hale to find out more about Thomas and his family – how many children he had, if there were servants living in the pub too, how long he and his family had been living in Little Hale, and so on. We know that there was at least one pub in the village before World War One. The house still exists, and is still called the Bowling Green, so we can compare photographs to see some of the changes in the village over the last 100 years.

Things to look at	Questions to ask
Clothes	What clothes are the people wearing? What does that tell us about them?
Mood	What expression is on their faces? What is the mood of the picture?
Pose	What are the people doing? Are they sitting, standing or working?
Background	What can you see in the background of the picture?
Black and white or colour	How does this affect the way we look at the photographs?
Reason	Why might the photograph have been taken? How does this affect how useful it is for an historian?

The Bowling Green public house, looking towards Great Hale and Heckington. Photograph taken around the turn of the century. Might this be Thomas Dickinson and his wife outside the pub?

Now it's your turn

1 What questions do you want to ask about this photograph?
2 Is there anything that surprises you about the photograph?
3 How useful is this photograph for telling us about Edwardian times?
4 Does the photograph agree with the information you have come across in other sources?

The Bowling Green public house, January 2010

Now it's your turn

1 What has changed between the two photographs?
2 What has stayed the same?
3 How useful do you think photographs are when studying local history?

Check your progress

I can identify similarities and differences between different periods of history using photographs.

I can begin to recognise the nature and extent of change and continuity using photographs.

I can make judgements about the extent and nature of change and continuity using photographs.

It's murder on the Orient Express

Objectives

By the end of this lesson you will be able to:

- explore life for the rich in the 1920s and 1930s

It was the most luxurious long distance rail journey in the history of travel. Royalty, aristocracy, the rich and the famous travelled regularly on the Orient Express. *Gourmet* chefs prepared exquisite meals. Staterooms and dining rooms on a par with famous hotels like the Ritz were all part of the experience.

Getting you thinking

The original Orient Express, started in 1889, was an ordinary international railway service. It has since become *synonymous* with luxury travel. In its heyday in the 1930s the Orient Express ran daily from Paris to Istanbul, a journey of over 3,000 km that took three nights.

Passengers would catch the boat train from London Victoria station, travel to Dover, cross the Channel by ferry and pick up their sleeping car in Calais. From there it was a short trip to Paris, where, without changing, the carriage would be added to the Orient Express – final destination Istanbul, then known as Constantinople. Just outside the station was the Pera Palas Hotel, built especially to accommodate travellers on the train, and still a five-star luxury hotel today.

Orient Express poster, 1895 (Credit: The Granger Collection, New York)

Gourmet: top quality
Synonymous: meaning the same as

If you were rich it seems that you could get away with anything. For example, the king of Bulgaria, an amateur engineer, insisted that he be allowed to drive the train through his country, which he did at *perilous* speeds. Tsar Nicholas II of Russia demanded that special cars be built for his visit to France before World War One.

The Orient Express was very luxurious. It was a short train, made up of just four sleeping-cars, plus dining cars and stateroom, with a baggage van at either end. Each carriage was specially built for the train, to the highest standard. Each passenger was allocated his or her own attendant. Each sleeping car had 10 wood-panelled compartments, with either one or two beds (one above the other) plus a washbasin – there were no baths or showers on board. The sleeper compartments converted for daytime use into a compact carpeted sitting room with sofa and small table.

Once the French president fell out of the train, to his great embarrassment. In 1929 the train was stuck in snow for five days, the inspiration for Agatha Christie's famous book *Murder on the Orient Express*.

Menu
Dinner

Steamed fresh salmon and spinach roulade, salmon tartar and eggplant pancake

Fillet of beef pickled with coarse salt, dill, juniper and coriander berries served raw thinly sliced and roasted with a tangy red wine sauce

Buttered baby vegetables

Potato cake

Choice of fine cheeses

Coffee

Sample menu, from the 2009 Venice Simplon Orient Express, based on 1930s Orient Express menus

Now it's your turn

1 Do you think people had to be rich to travel on the Orient Express?
2 What does the Orient Express tell us about society in the 1920s and 1930s?
3 What questions would you need to ask to find out more about the travellers on the Orient Express?

Extension work

There is a famous 1974 feature film *Murder on the Orient Express*. Watch the film, and assess how accurate it is in terms of historical reality. Make a list of the pros and cons of using film as historical evidence.

Check your progress

I can ask questions about the past.
I can suggest my own enquiry questions when investigating historical problems and issues.
I can conduct historical enquiries by defining and refining enquiry questions and beginning to evaluate the process.

Perilous: very dangerous

Could you live on £1 a week?

Objectives

By the end of this lesson you will be able to:

- discover how hard it was to live on the average wage before World War One
- find out what some people thought about this at the time

Make a list of what you spend your money on. How much of it is 'essential' and how much is spent on extras? How easy is it to get extra money out of your parents if you want a treat, or money for a school trip, for example? What would your life be like if you never had any money at all?

Getting you thinking

In 1909 a group of middle-class ladies began a study of 42 families in London. The families were not the poorest of the poor. They were dustmen, policemen and bus conductors – people regarded as having respectable jobs. They all earned around £1* a week – the standard wage at the time – if they worked every day. The middle-class ladies expected to find waste and extravagance, the men drinking away their wages and the women wasting money on fancy foods. The result was a famous book published in 1913.

* The nearest equivalent in 2008 was around about £100 per week.

A slum in Westminster, central London at the beginning of the twentieth century

Pauper: someone with no money and no job

Here is a typical diet for a manual labourer in 1905, who earned just under £1 a week. He had a wife and three children:

> Breakfast: bread, tea, butter
> Dinner: fish (probably herrings), bread, tea
> Tea: bread, butter, onions, tea
> Supper: none

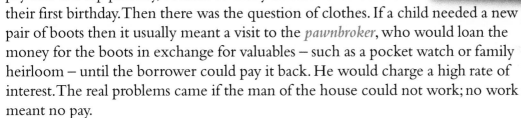

ROUND ABOUT A POUND A WEEK
Maud Pember Reeves
Introduction by Sally Alexander

'As disturbing now as when it first shocked complacent, moralising, late Edwardian England'
THE TIMES

Most of the income would be spent on food, but there was also rent to pay – often nearly half a man's wages. Next there would be burial insurance to pay. It was regarded as a great disgrace to bury children in a *pauper's* grave, so each week a family would pay that as a top priority, because so many children died before their first birthday. Then there was the question of clothes. If a child needed a new pair of boots then it usually meant a visit to the *pawnbroker*, who would loan the money for the boots in exchange for valuables – such as a pocket watch or family heirloom – until the borrower could pay it back. He would charge a high rate of interest. The real problems came if the man of the house could not work; no work meant no pay.

In an attempt to improve conditions, trade unions grew bigger, bargaining with employers for better wages and better conditions. Strikes were common. The Labour Party was set up to represent working men in parliament, although at the time MPs were unpaid, so people had to be rich to stand for parliament. Friendly societies and 'savings clubs' helped people cope with bad times. And the Liberal government introduced new laws to help workers, including old age pensions and unemployment insurance.

Extension work

Find out about the Liberal government's reforms 1906–1914 that tried to make life easier for working people.

Now it's your turn

1 The author of *Round About A Pound A Week* states that however hard you try, however you shop or cook, it is absolutely impossible to live decently or healthily on £1 a week. Why, then, do you think wages were so low?
2 What types of food are missing from the diet quoted above? How does it affect people if they don't eat these foods regularly?
3 Why were working-class people so afraid of growing old or falling ill at this time?
4 What was done about the problem?

Check your progress

I can describe some aspects of life for poor working people in 1900.
I can describe some of the ways people tried to improve living conditions for working-class people.
I can talk about what working-class people were most afraid of, and give reasons.

Pawnbroker: shopkeeper who loaned money to borrowers who had something valuable to leave as a deposit

Just how friendly were friendly societies?

Objectives

By the end of this lesson you will be able to:

- find out about workers' attempts to help themselves through difficult times
- decide how effective those attempts were

It is estimated that by the 1900s about 4.5 million people, nearly all working men, belonged to friendly societies registered with the government. There may have been another 4.5 million members of unregistered societies. That means about 9–10 million workers were regularly paying into a friendly society of one kind or another. Why?

The Hearts of Oak Benefit Society certificate, 1869

Getting you thinking

Friendly societies began in the 18th century. Workers got together to help each other out in times of need. A weekly subscription entitled members to a regular payment if they were too sick to work, or to pay for their funeral. Some societies also paid in effect an old age pension once members were too old to work. How much was paid out depended on how much a worker had paid in; for instance, in 1900, the Manchester Unity of Odd Fellows paid out the following rates:

Subscription:
6 pence a week.

Sickness benefit:
9 shillings a week for the first 12 months
4 shillings and 6 pence a week after that

Death Benefit:
£9 on death of a member
£4 10 shillings on death of a member's wife

Subscription: regular weekly payment   **Benefits:** payments   **Pauper funeral:** no coffin and no marked grave, paid for by the Poor Law   **Frivolity:** lighthearted enjoyment

Other societies had lower subscriptions – perhaps 2 pence or 3 pence a week and paid lower benefits. Some 'clubs' as they were called merely provided death *benefits* – enough to prevent the dreaded *pauper funeral*.

'Old' money	Decimal equivalent
1d	0.4p
1 shilling [12d]	5p
10 shillings	50p
£1	£1

Friendly societies also played a part in people's social life. Such occasions were opportunities for fun and *frivolity*, something to take workers' minds away from the daily toil. They would also hold fetes and garden parties in the summer months, to raise funds to make sure each society had enough money to pay its members.

Friendly societies do not often figure in history books – authors tend to focus on what governments did. Historians have argued about the impact of friendly societies. Membership was huge, but very few members were women. Once members stopped paying their subscription they lost out on benefits, so if a worker was in irregular employment or money

Members of the Manchester Unity of Odd Fellows, a local friendly society, practise for a parade in 1939

was tight then they might lose their *entitlement* at the very time they needed most help. Low-paid workers found it hard to make regular payments, although most were determined to find the penny or two pence a week needed to keep up the death benefit payments; this shows a real determination to help themselves in times of difficulty. Friendly societies were regarded as a good influence on workers and as a training ground for democracy; all posts were elected, and the money had to be carefully controlled. Some historians now argue that friendly societies were more important than the Poor Law or the *workhouse* for helping families in need. What do you think?

Now it's your turn

1 Why do you think so many people belonged to friendly societies?
2 Why were people so afraid of a pauper funeral?
3 Do you agree that friendly societies were a training ground for democracy?
4 Why do you think friendly societies rarely appear in history textbooks?

Check your progress

I can describe what friendly societies were.

I can talk about the benefits they provided and some of the limitations.

I can decide on the importance of friendly societies in history, and give reasons

Entitlement: claim   Workhouse: the poor had to go into the workhouse to get help from the Poor Law authorities. Conditions were worse in the workhouse than outside.

What was life like in a mining village?

Objectives

By the end of this lesson you will be able to:

- explore the differences within a working-class community around the time of World War One

Just look around you. Doesn't it make you think how different we all are? Everyone may be wearing the same school uniform, be roughly the same age, doing the same piece of work. Yet we all look very different from each other, and respond to situations in different ways.

Here is one person's account of the village in which she grew up. Everyone in the village lived in a similar house, with no toilet or running water. All the men were coal miners.
All faced real problems in their daily lives.

Miners' cottages from Hetton-le-Hole, reconstructed at Beamish open air museum, Durham

Feckless: wasteful, useless
Prudish: easily offended by matters relating to sex

Getting you thinking

Winifred Foley was born in 1914, and grew up in a coal-mining village in the Forest of Dean, in Gloucestershire. Here she describes her village:

…in our village at that time the few feckless, filthy and friendly families tended to live at one end; the prim, prudish and prosperous families at the other. Between these two extremes lived a group of middling families, and this was where we fitted in.

Here, in the centre of the village, lived a dozen or so families, not yet well off enough to move from their ancestral poverty, nor yet driven into complete squalor. The cottages – two-up, two-down, with a back-kitchen-cum-coal-house, had large gardens … Here were many children, but efforts were made to keep them clothed and fed, and even educated. Pigs were kept and fowls.

We were never anything but poor … Coal was no problem, as every working miner had an allowance of twelve hundredweight [12 × 50kg] a month. The wonders of gas and electricity we only knew of second-hand from girls on holiday from service. Candles and paraffin lamps lit our home. Many's the time I've been sent around trying to borrow 'a stump of candle.' Come to that, I was often sent for a 'pinch of tea', ' a lick of marge' [margarine], 'a screw of sugar', 'a sliver of soap', or 'a snarl of bread.' No one was ever optimistic enough to try to borrow money.

When I think of the 'slums' at the feckless end, the colour that comes to mind is grey. The children's skins were grimed grey with dirt … the interiors of the cottages were mostly grey … they scarcely saw soap and water from one week to the next…

Life was wonderful except for one constant nagging irritation: hunger.

Winifred Foley, 'Full Hearts and Empty Bellies'

Now it's your turn

1 Do you think Winifred was successful when she was sent around to borrow things? Why?
2 How does Winifred distinguish between the people in her village? Does she think she is better or worse than other people in the village?
3 Winifred called her autobiography 'Full Hearts and Empty Bellies'. What impression of her childhood is she trying to give by using a title like this?
4 Winifred's autobiography was first written in 1975, fifty years after the events she is describing. Do you think that makes the book more reliable, or less reliable?

Check your progress

I can use a source to talk about life in a coal-mining village.
I can talk about some of the differences in the ways people lived.
I can talk about some of the problems mining families faced, and how they dealt with them..

Squalor: dirt, filth
Allowance: regular amount

What was it like to be unemployed in the 1930s?

Objectives

By the end of this lesson you will be able to:

- find out what it was like to be unemployed in the 1930s
- use the evidence to reach a conclusion

After the Wall Street Crash in 1929 (see page 62) virtually the whole world went into a *depression*. Millions lost their jobs. In Britain nearly 3 million men were out of work.

Getting you thinking

When I first lost my job it didn't seem too bad. I would wake up in the morning and go to get up as usual. Then I would realise I could have a nice lie-in. It was like being on holiday. That didn't last though. The days went by and I got desperate. I cycled all over the place, and I stood in queues with scores of men knowing that only a couple of us would be lucky and get work. Many a time I was outside a factory gate at six o' clock in the morning, hoping to catch the foreman's eye. It was useless. I am 58 you see, and no one wanted a man that age. After a time I gave up really trying...

Source 1 *An engineer in the 1930s*

Unemployed people demonstrate in Oxford Circus, London, 1938.

Depression: economic slump with high unemployment
Dole: unemployment pay

The 1930s were hard times. The dole queues meant no jobs for married women. Although my mum could read and write, she was only able to get cleaning jobs at the big houses. My mother used to clean at one large house near the bottom of Perry Hill Road; she would earn half a crown for cleaning the whole house. The men also suffered, no work and no state benefit at that time. They would take any sort of work, odd jobs, gardening, labouring, just to earn a few shillings to put food on the table...

Source 2 *Gladys Jones remembers growing up in Birmingham in the 1930s*

Jarrow is a town in the north-east of England. The main industry was shipbuilding. In 1935 the shipyard was closed. Overnight 80 per cent of the town became unemployed.

In 1931 everything went bankrupt, and we in Jarrow had to suffer for it. Often my wife and I went without a meal on Sunday in order to feed the children. We patched all our clothes. In the town 156 shops were closed or empty.

Source 3 *A description of Jarrow written in the 1930s*

There was no work. No one had a job except a few railwaymen, officials, the workers in the co-operative stores, and a few workmen who went out of the town...

Source 4 *Ellen Wilkinson, MP for Jarrow*

Now it's your turn

1 What effects did unemployment have on people in the 1930s?
2 In what ways do the four sources support each other in what they say?
3 Which of the four sources do you find most reliable? Why?
4 Make a list of questions you would like to ask the engineer quoted in source 1.

Extension work

1 Find out more about Jarrow in the 1930s, and what the town did to try to make things better for the people there.
2 Find out more about Ellen Wilkinson, who was one of only four women Labour MPs at the time.

Check your progress

I can use sources to find out about unemployment in the 1930s.
I can compare historical sources to see if they agree, and make judgements on their reliability.
I can build up a picture of what life was like for unemployed people in the 1930s.

Benefit: regular payments by the state in times of need

Were the 1930s bad for everybody?

Objectives

By the end of this lesson you will be able to:

- explore different interpretations of the 1930s

- explore how the viewpoints, claims or judgements in one interpretation differ from those in another

Ever since the 1930s, historians, politicians, filmmakers and authors have been making interpretations of the 1930s. This lesson gives you the opportunity to examine some of these, and to explore their similarities and differences.

Semi-detached houses in north London, around 1930

Means test: a test of income which determines who is eligible for benefits
Abundant: lots and lots

The inter-war years have been seen as a time of horrors: dole queues, means tests, hunger marches, poverty, inequality, malnutrition, disease and despair. There is abundant evidence for this view … JB Priestley said that places like Jarrow looked far worse than war-torn towns he had visited in northern France. After the slump, so many smoke-belching textile mills went out of business that Blackburn began to look clean … Historians, however, have long since revised this grim picture. Prices fell sharply between the wars and average incomes rose by about a third … Three million houses were built during the 1930s, a bungalow could be purchased for £225 and a semi for £450. The middle class also bought radiograms, telephones, three-piece suites, electric cookers, vacuum cleaners and golf clubs. They ate Kellogg's Corn Flakes, drove to Odeon cinemas in Austin Sevens (costing £135 by 1930) and smoked Craven A cigarettes, cork-tipped 'to prevent sore throats'. The depression spawned a consumer boom…

Piers Brendon, reviewing 'We Danced All Night: A Social History of Britain Between the Wars' by Martin Pugh (the Guardian, 5 July 2008)

The period between the wars was one of contrasts; mass unemployment, dole queues, hunger marches and the means test; on the other hand it was a time of higher wages for those lucky enough to have jobs, a boom in housing, a rapid increase in car ownership and the availability of cheaper consumer goods. To a large extent, an individual's experience during the period depended on who they were, where they lived and what their occupation was.

Black Country Living Museum website

The sheer magnitude of the problem was staggering – at the depth of the slump in September 1932 between six and seven million people were dependent on the 'dole' – men who could not find work, plus their wives and families. Not just for a week or two or a month or two – in Wigan, for instance, four or five thousand miners stayed continuously unemployed over eight years. During the thirties one in three of all workers was out of work for some part of the time, many of them for long periods. The coal they mined, or the products they helped manufacture, could not be sold, so there was no work for them until 'times got better'.

Ian Martin, 'From Workhouse to Welfare: The development of the Welfare State' (1971)

Now it's your turn

1 In what ways do the three sources above agree about the 1930s?
2 In what ways do the three sources disagree about the 1930s?
3 Can you suggest reasons for the disagreements?
4 Which of the interpretations support the information on the spreads on pages 184–185?
5 What image of the 1930s would you give if you were writing your own interpretation of the period?

Check your progress

I can compare different ways in which people have described the 1930s.

I can suggest some reasons why historians offer different interpretations of the 1930s.

I can reach my own judgement on the 1930s by comparing sources.of

Houses for everyone?

Objectives

By the end of this lesson you will be able to:

- explain why there was a housing shortage after World War Two
- understand what the government did about the housing shortage
- understand how people felt about the new houses

Around 160,000 *prefabs* were built in the UK after World War Two. They were intended as temporary homes to replace those damaged by bombing. They were made in a factory, using aluminium from shot-down aircraft, and put together on site, on a concrete base. Some had plywood frames. They usually had two bedrooms, came complete with a fitted kitchen and bathroom, and had a fire that heated the house and provided hot water. They often had a large garden. They were very popular.

Getting you thinking

What did the prefabs' occupants like about them? These were temporary buildings, so they had thin walls and poor insulation – one former occupant remembers scraping the frost off the inside of the windows on winter mornings. But many of the houses that people lived in before the war were even colder. Read the sources on the right to find out what people who lived in the prefabs remember about them.

A prefab house, built as temporary housing after World War Two

Prefabs: houses made in sections, and delivered to be erected
Demolition: being knocked down

I was born and brought up in a prefab. Our prefab was so warm and cosy. It broke our hearts when we had to be moved out and rehoused. We had so much storage space. We had the luxury of having a fully fitted kitchen then. We were very privileged to have all that, the fridge, copper boiler for our washing, and cooker. When we left the prefab every thing was still in working order … It really was a lovely place.

Marlene Hale, 'Prefab Palaces', BBC South East Wales

My Mom, brother and I were amongst the first people to live in prefabs on Calder Road [in Edinburgh.] We lived at No 547. Mom loved the many built-in closets, cabinets and drawers and swore it must have been designed by a female since males would never have thought of this feature.

Lillian Young

Safe as prefabs – Grade II listing preserves Second World War relics

The UK's biggest surviving estate of post-second world war prefab houses has been saved – in part – from possible demolition after the DCSF listed the bungalows as being of particular historic interest. Six of the homes in Catford, South-East London, have been granted Grade II listed status. Some locals had wanted all 187 houses, along with the estate's accompanying tin-roofed prefab church, to receive official protection.

The Guardian, 17 March 2009

Now it's your turn

1 Why was there such a demand for houses after World War Two?
2 Why, in your opinion, did people find prefabs so attractive to live in?
3 What are the disadvantages of living in prefabs?
4 Some of the residents of Catford want to preserve their estate of prefabs. Do you think they should succeed? Why?

Check your progress

I can say what prefab houses were like, and why they were built.

I can use sources to find out about what the prefabs' occupants thought of them.

I can decide on the historical importance of prefabs, and give reasons.

The swinging sixties: pop music

In July 1957, Britain's prime minister, Harold MacMillan, said in a speech that 'most of our people have never had it so good.' He could have been talking about young people in the 1960s. Young people suddenly had money to spend on whatever they wanted, and developed a culture all of their own.

Getting you thinking

Sergeant Pepper's Lonely Hearts Club Band by the Beatles, 1967

Ever since 1936, there had been a weekly 'hit parade', or chart, listing the current best-selling music. Originally, it referred to sales of sheet music. It wasn't until the 1950s that it began to refer to recorded music, sold as vinyl *LPs* and singles.. By the 1960s, radio stations like Radio Luxembourg and 'pirate' unlicensed stations (like Radio Caroline from

LPs: long-playing records

1964) were broadcasting pop music 24 hours a day. The BBC responded by setting up Radio One in 1967, specifically aimed at young people. On television, 'Top of the Pops' was first broadcast in 1964, running continuously until 2006. Each week there was a new chart to celebrate.

Young people spent money on records – who was 'number one' in the hit parade was front-page news. For the first time, footballers and pop stars were major celebrities, and they set the trends in fashion, in behaviour and in ideas.

In the mid-sixties, hippies began to appear. Based partly on Indian religious ideas, and the use of drugs such as marijuana, their lifestyle was a reaction against work and the values of their parents' generation. Everything was shared: groups of people lived together in communes and aimed to make the world a 'better place'. Just a few people lived the lifestyle, but it was very influential.

Perhaps the high spot of the sixties music scene was the Woodstock Festival in New York State, in August 1969. It is estimated that 400,000 people attended the three-day event and watched most of the world's leading performers. Bands like the Beatles who were asked to perform and declined afterwards bitterly regretted not being there. It was the first major free pop festival.

Other influential musicians from the 1960s you might like to explore include Bob Dylan, The Rolling Stones, Jimi Hendrix, The Supremes, The Beach Boys, Simon & Garfunkel, Elvis Presley, The Doors and Joan Baez.

Now it's your turn

1 How has the nature of pop music changed between 1963 and 1970?
2 How has the appearance of pop musicians changed over the same period?
3 Why might those pop stars who didn't perform at Woodstock regret not being there?
4 In what ways were hippies different from the rest of the population? Do you think that matters?

Check your progress

I can describe some features of music in the 1960s.
I can describe some of the changes in young people's attitudes
I can compare the 1960s with the present day, and see what has changed and what has stayed the same.

The swinging sixties: women

Objectives

By the end of this lesson you will be able to:

- examine how life changed for women during the 1960s

In the 1960s there was a real change in the status and image of women. This was brought about by women themselves pushing for change through the *feminist movement*, as much as by men changing laws.

Getting you thinking

The 1960s was the first decade in which all young women received full-time secondary education up to the age of 15. This led to a huge increase in the number of women attending universities. Many more women were working as teachers, nurses and secretaries, as well as breaking into areas such as engineering, architecture and the civil service.

There were legal changes too. In 1967 married women were granted similar rights to their husband in the marital home. The 1967 Abortion Act legalised abortion and in 1969 the divorce law was reformed so that either party could sue for divorce. The *predominant* image of women shifted from being that of wife and mother to that of a young, free, single girl.

The miniskirt seemed to express it all. Young girls did not want to dress like their mothers; they seized the chance to express their individuality. New fabrics in bright colours added to the excitement of the new fashions. The wider availability of the contraceptive pill (invented in 1961, but not available on the NHS until 1974), a far more reliable method of family planning than those previously available, allowed women to be more relaxed about sex and family planning.

In June 1968, 850 sewing machine operators at Ford's car plant in Dagenham, East London, went on strike for equal pay with men doing the same job. They were making car seat covers. At the time the women were paid about 85 per cent of men's wages. Despite never having been on strike before, or even all being union members, the strike was successful. Within days the strike had spread to all Ford plants in the UK, bringing car production nearly to a standstill. After three weeks on strike, the women agreed a deal where they were to be paid 92 per cent of men's wages, and went back to work. The strike is regarded as one of the key reasons why the Labour government introduced the Equal Pay Act in 1970, making it illegal to pay women less than men if they were doing the same job.

Women as a percentage of those in higher education

1929 28%
1959 25%
1989 40%

Women as a percentage of the workforce

1911 33%
1951 31%
1970 35%

Feminist movement: women trying to make their lives better
Predominant: most influential

Women protesting for equal pay, mid-1960s

Other influential women from the 1960s you might like to explore
include Mary Quant, Twiggy, Coco Chanel, Katharine Hepburn,
Dorothy Hodgkin, Germaine Greer, Billie Jean King, Barbara Castle,
Mother Teresa and Sirimavo Bandaranaike.

Now it's your turn

1 In what ways did life for many
women change during the
1960s?
2 Does that mean life changed
for all women? Explain your
answer.
3 What, in your opinion, was the
biggest change in the 1960s?
Why?

Check your progress

I can suggest some causes of the changes
in the lives of women in the 1960s.

I can describe some key events and
changes in the 1960s that changed
women's lives.

I can compare the 1960s with the present
day to see what has changed and what has
stayed the same.

The swinging sixties: technology

Objectives

By the end of this lesson you will be able to:

- explore the changes in technology during the 1960s

The 1960s saw the invention or introduction of many things we now take for granted. Prime Minister Harold Wilson talked about 'the white heat of technology' and its impact on Britain's industry. Technology was going to make Britain rich! It was the time many British families bought their first car, or took their first cheap overseas holiday. It was the time when England won the World Cup, and Neil Armstrong and Buzz Aldrin landed on the moon. It was an exciting and optimistic time – technology was going to solve all the problems of the world.

Getting you thinking

The 1960s was an exciting time to grow up. The first electric main-line trains were running from London to Scotland, cutting journey times significantly. New motorways seemed to be opening all the time. Colour television with more than two channels meant a choice of viewing – there were now three or four channels to choose from. There were new radio stations and many homes now had a telephone so you didn't have to walk to the nearest telephone kiosk in order to call a friend. There was change everywhere.

Benidorm

Benidorm is near Alicante on the Costa Blanca. In the early 1960s it was just a small fishing port. The old church is now surrounded by more than 1,000 hotels, bars, restaurants and apartments. In the 1960s package holidays to the Costa Blanca started to become popular. Alicante airport opened in 1967 and this was the biggest contributing factor to the success of Benidorm as a holiday resort. Modern jets made flying cheap enough for the ordinary family to enjoy a holiday abroad. Benidorm was the model upon which all other holiday resorts were based. Cheap accommodation – often better than the houses they lived in – cheap food and booze, and lots of sunshine and beaches made the package holiday to Spain or Greece ideal. In 1977 Benidorm alone entertained over 12 million visitors!

Barbie dolls, Etch A Sketch, Hula Hoops, Lego and Twister were all popular toys. *Perry Mason*, *Doctor Who*, *Lassie*, *Flipper*, *Steptoe and Son*, *The Man from U.N.C.L.E.*, *Coronation Street* and *The Monkees* were all watched by millions of people on television.

One of the biggest events in the 1960s was the first moon landing, watched by millions of people around the world on their new black–and–white televisions.

- Who was the first man to walk on the moon, and when did it happen? What were his famous first words?

Other new technology from the time you might like to explore includes the cash dispenser, communication satellites, the personal computer, fibre optics, the heart pacemaker, the portable calculator, the tape cassette, weather satellites, colour television, and the transistor radio.

Now it's your turn

1. What, in your opinion, were the biggest changes brought about by technology?
2. What impact might foreign travel and cheap holidays have had on people in Britain?
3. Why do you think Harold Wilson was so excited by 'the white heat of technology'?

Check your progress

I can talk about some of the new technologies that appeared in the 1960s.
I can describe some ways in which technology changed people's lives.
I can describe some other changes in people's lives in the 1960s, and suggest some causes of these changes.

Objectives

By the end of this lesson you will be able to:

- explore the issue of migration in the 1960s

In 1968 a Conservative MP, Enoch Powell, made a speech in Birmingham that became known as the 'Rivers of Blood' speech. In it, he argued that continued unlimited immigration from the Commonwealth would lead to race riots and increased racial tension. His speech was a response to the 1968 Race Relations Act, which made it *illegal* to refuse housing, employment, or public services to a person on the grounds of colour, race, ethnic or national origins.

So why had immigration become such a sensitive issue in Britain?

Getting you thinking

People have always migrated to Britain. They have usually been made welcome. After World War Two, Britain faced a shortage of workers. Advertisements were placed in countries like Jamaica, inviting men to come and work. The first group, who arrived aboard the Empire Windrush in 1948, were mainly single men looking to settle in Britain and then pay for their wives to join them. In the 1950s employers also began recruiting in India and Pakistan. All these migrants, from the former Empire, had full British citizenship and every right to come and live in Britain. Most of the migrants took low-paid, unskilled jobs that no one else would do. Therefore they tended to live in the poorer, more run-down parts of cities; that was all they could afford. This sometimes led to resentment from white people who were less well off; they felt they could no longer afford houses in these areas.

In an attempt to control the number of immigrants, the Conservative government introduced the Commonwealth Immigrants Act in 1962, which restricted the right of people to come and settle here. Only those with *employment vouchers* issued by the government could enter the UK. The 1968 Commonwealth Immigrants Act further limited this right.

A *Punch* cartoon suggests the different ways immigrants might view both Britain and Jamaica

Illegal: against the law
Employment vouchers: permission to work

In fact, throughout the 20th century, levels of emigration – people leaving this country to live overseas – had nearly always exceeded immigration, as these figures show:

decade	emigration	immigration
1920–29	3,960,000	2,590,000
1930–39	2,273,000	2,361,000
1940–49	590,000	240,000
1950–59	1,327,000	676,000
1960–69	1,916,000	1,243,000
1970–79	2,554,000	1,900,000

Figures taken from Michael Lynch, 'An Introduction to Modern British History 1900-1999'

British people went to live and work in countries like the USA, Canada, Australia, New Zealand, South Africa, Kenya, Rhodesia and parts of South America. For many years you could get an *assisted passage* to Australia or New Zealand for only £10. The father of one of this book's authors applied to go to Australia in 1960 when the coal mine where he worked closed down. His wife, however, refused to leave her family and go to the other side of the world; in those days, before the internet and cheap airfares, it seemed much further away than it does today.

Other events and people from the time you might like to explore include the Bristol Bus Boycott (1962); the Notting Hill Riots (1958); the expulsion of Asians from Uganda (1972); TV sitcom 'Till Death Us Do Part' (1965); Basil D'Oliveira (1968-69) and Enoch Powell.

Now it's your turn

1 In what ways did immigration cause tensions during the 1960s?
2 List all the ways you think immigration has changed life in Britain.
3 Do you think passing laws changes people's attitudes to race and immigration?

Check your progress

I can begin to suggest some causes of the tensions over immigration.
I can begin to recognise the nature and extent of diversity in the 1960s.
I can make a judgment about the nature and extent of diversity in the 1960s, and give reasons.

Assisted passage: cheap fare, subsidised by the country you are going to, to encourage immigrants

Never had it so good?

The last four lessons have all focused on the 1960s, a time of great change in Britain. They have presented you with a lot of information and ideas about the time. People suddenly had a lot more *disposable wealth*, and they spent it on consumer goods and holidays, as well as on buying houses and cars.

'Go to work on an egg', a famous advertising campaign from the 1960s

Disposable wealth: money to spend on non-essential items

Getting you thinking

What do you already know about the 1960s?

Draw a timeline from 1960–1970, like this one:

1960 61 62 63 64 65 66 67 68 69 70

Make it a big one. On it mark each of the events you have found out about over the last four lessons. Colour-code it using one colour for political; one colour for social; one colour for economic; and one colour for cultural events.

Do you agree with Harold MacMillan's statement (page 190) that 'most of our people have never had it so good'?

Does your timeline support the argument that the 1960s were a time of great change?

Do you have enough information to agree or disagree with this statement? What else would you need to know? Make a list of the information you still need to be able to answer this question.

Now it's your turn

What have you found most fascinating about the 1960s? What would you like to explore more? With a partner make a list of questions you have about the 1960s. You might like to find out more about some of the issues you have already looked at in this unit, or you might want to explore something new.

Once you have your question, how are you going to set about finding the answer? Most historians research their topic, producing notes, thoughts and random jottings that cover anything they come across that seems relevant.

Remember you need to be able to *substantiate* your ideas and arguments – you really need several pieces of evidence supporting each other before you can really say something is likely to be true. And of

course you will probably find plenty of *conflicting* evidence. If that is the case, which evidence will you believe, and why? You will need all your powers as an historian to come to a reasoned conclusion.

Once you have done your research and found what you think is a convincing answer to your question, how are you going to present your work? You could produce an essay, a PowerPoint presentation, an oral report, a newspaper report or a TV or radio script. Which one you choose will depend on both the question you have asked, the evidence you have discovered, and your intended audience. Is this work to be presented to your teacher, your class or the school website? Each type of presentation will influence what evidence and ideas you can use.

Check your progress

I can ask questions about the past, and use sources to find answers.
I can suggest my own enquiry questions using historical sources to help me.
I can carry out a historical enquiry into the question, and reach some conclusions based on the evidence.

Substantiate: *confirm or support an idea*
Conflicting: *contradictory, inconsistent, saying different things*

How should Margaret Thatcher be remembered?

Margaret Thatcher is the only woman to have served as a party leader in Britain and the only woman to have become prime minister. She won three elections in a row – in 1979, 1983 and 1987 – and held continuous office for 11 years, from 1979 to 1990, longer than any other prime minister of the 20th century. Few, if any, prime ministers have aroused such controversy as Margaret Thatcher.

A portrait of Margaret Thatcher

Getting you thinking

Margaret Thatcher entered politics in 1959 when she became Conservative MP for Finchley. In 1970 she was appointed secretary of state for education in Edward Heath's government; she gained *renown* as 'Margaret Thatcher, milk snatcher' for ending the provision of free school milk. She became leader of the Conservative Party in 1975, and on 4 May 1979 became Britain's first female prime minister.

Monetarist policies: controlling the economy by limiting how much money there is available to spend

It was a time of rising prices, high unemployment and slow economic growth. She was determined to reverse this with her *monetarist policies*. In other words, she believed the nation had to pay its way and balance its books. So she opposed trade unions' demands for wage increases for their members; government spending on public services – such as health, education and policing – was cut; state-owned companies, such as British Telecom, British Airways, Rolls Royce and British Steel, were sold off to private business to raise money. Such policies initially made her very unpopular, but the 1982 Falklands War and later economic recovery strengthened her position.

On 2 April 1982 Argentina invaded the Falkland Islands. On 5 April the British Navy set sail for the Falklands. British troops landed in late May and fighting continued until Argentina surrendered on 14 June 1982. Thatcher's personal popularity was greatly boasted by winning the war, and the Conservative Party won the 1983 general election with a huge majority.

In her second term Margaret Thatcher continued to take a hard line against trade unions. *Sympathy strikes* (in support of strikes in other industries) were banned and union leaders had to ballot members on strike action. Unions were also made responsible for the actions of their members. The government took a firm stand against individual disputes; the miners' strike that began in 1984 lasted for 12 months without success.

A firm line was also taken against the Soviet Union and Thatcher's tough talking gained her the nickname 'The Iron Lady', although her views changed after Mikhail Gorbachev became the new Soviet leader in 1985 (see page 144).

Re-elected for an unprecedented third term in 1987, the following years proved difficult for Margaret Thatcher. The introduction of the Community Charge (Poll Tax) in April 1989 in Scotland, which charged people local government taxes per head rather than per house, severely damaged her reputation and led to public demonstrations.

In November 1990 her leadership of the Conservative Party was challenged and on 28 November she resigned as prime minister.

Now it's your turn

1 One historian stated that 'if she had not won the Falklands War Mrs Thatcher would have served only one term as prime minister and been considered a failure.' To decide whether you agree with this statement, what else would you need to find out that is not covered in this lesson?
2 Mrs Thatcher was the longest-serving prime minister of the 20th century. Does this also make her the greatest prime minister?
3 How should we remember Mrs Thatcher?

Check your progress

I can decide if Mrs Thatcher was a great prime minister.
I can decide on things I need to find out in order to make a historical judgment on Mrs Thatcher.
I can come up with my own criteria for judging Mrs Thatcher.

Renown: *fame*
Sympathy strike: *strikes in support of other industries on strike*

What does it mean to be British today?

Objectives

By the end of this lesson you will be able to:

- explore the idea of 'Britishness'
- select exhibits to go into a new 'British' museum

Norman Tebbitt, a Conservative politician, once argued that the test of being British was which cricket team you would support in an international match – that of the country you were born in, or England? What would you set as a test for 'Britishness?'

Participants in a sponsored run in the 2000s

Iconic: very famous and significant

Getting you thinking

Gordon Brown, who became British prime minister in 2007, supported suggestions that there should be a 'British day' to 'focus on the things that bring us together … whatever our backgrounds'. The French have Bastille Day; the Americans have Thanksgiving Day.

Several suggestions have been made for 'British Day':

VE Day	8 May
Oak Apple Day	29 May
D Day	6 June
Democracy Day	7 June
Battle of Waterloo	17 June
Wilberforce Day	24 August
Battle of Hastings	14 October
Trafalgar Day	21 October
Armistice Day	11 November

Which of these days would you choose? Or are there any others you would choose instead?

In 2007 plans for a new museum of British history were proposed. It was suggested that the new museum would focus not just on how a museum could tell the story of British history, but also on celebrating the great British values that have shaped our culture, politics and society.

Where do you think this new museum should be built? Should it be built in London, the capital city, or somewhere else? Where you decide to build this museum sends out as powerful a message as what you decide to put in it.

Now it's your turn

1   You have been asked to design the first gallery for the new museum of British history. It is the first thing that visitors will see as they enter the museum, so it is important that you get it right! There is only space for ten exhibits, and their function is to explain to visitors what it is to be British. Working in groups, produce a list of ten exhibits for your display. Once you have an agreed list, you then need to decide in which order you want to display your exhibits. Which will be the most effective order for visitors to see the ten items? How you arrange the exhibits will affect the visitors' experience of the gallery.

2   Think back over all the topics you have studied in history in Key Stage 3. Which do you think deserve to be seen as *'iconic'*? Which of them help to define 'Britishness?' Which have, in your opinion, made us what we are today? How many political items should you include and how many cultural, social and/or economic items should you include?

3   Each exhibit also needs a caption to explain what it is and why you have chosen it. Museum policy is to have captions of no more than 100 words. So you need to think carefully about how you say things as well as what you say.

4   Finally, what are you going to call your gallery? You can't just call it 'the first gallery,' or 'an introduction to the museum'. Devise a title for your gallery that tells visitors exactly what it does.

Check your progress

I can decide on some historical events that define 'Britishness'.
I can think about what objects to include in a new museum of British history.
I can think about how to display these objects, and write captions to go with them.

Feed the world!

In autumn 1984 a BBC TV camera crew went to Northern Ethiopia, to film a famine. This was after several years with little or no rainfall in the country. Over 8 million people were starving, and over 1 million are estimated to have died in that year.

The famine was made worse by civil war; several parts of the country were fighting to break away from Ethiopia and set themselves up as independent countries. At first the Ethiopian government denied there was a famine; then it sent food only to government-controlled areas. Finally, the BBC film was shown on the evening news; the pictures of starving children made an immediate impact.

Band Aid

Getting you thinking

Watching the news broadcast was an Irish pop star, Bob Geldof, from the group The Boomtown Rats. He was so moved by the pictures that he immediately began working on a record to raise money to help the famine victims. He contacted lots of other pop stars and the result was Band Aid's hit single, 'Feed the World', which became the Christmas number one, and raised around £8 million, all of which went to Ethiopia as aid. This was followed in July 1985 by Live Aid, two massive concerts held in London and Philadelphia, USA at the same time and shown live on TV. Over 400 million people watched the concerts live around the world; around $150 million was raised for the relief work in Ethiopia.

At the same time, the television news item stirred up governments all around the world to help. The Royal Air Force used Hercules transport planes to drop supplies to remote regions; the USA, Germany, the USSR, Canada and many other countries sent relief supplies. Millions of people donated money to charities such as Oxfam; in the UK over £5 million was donated by ordinary people in just three days.

Throughout 1982 and 1983, Western governments had been reluctant to help starving Ethiopians, because the country was ruled by a communist military leader. They feared that any money they gave to Ethiopia would be used to buy weapons instead of food. They argued that any food they sent would be used to feed Ethiopian troops fighting the civil war in Eritrea and Tigre provinces rather than the starving. It was only after the famine became news that governments began to act.

Similar crises have happened many times since, including the tsunami in the Pacific Ocean in 2004, when over 1 million people are said to have died. Each time, people have given millions of pounds to help victims, following appeals by charity organisations.

Bob Geldof was made a knight – Sir Bob Geldof – for his work with Band Aid and Live Aid.

> Feed the World,
> Feed the World,
> Let them Know its
>   Christmastime again.
>
> *Lyrics from Band Aid's 'Feed the World'*

Now it's your turn

1 'Band Aid and Live Aid show that people are always willing to help those worse off than themselves.' Do you agree?
2 'The response to the famine in Ethiopia shows how much influence television has on us today'. Do you agree?

Extension work

Can you identify other areas where you think television has had a major impact on people's lives?

Check your progress

I can describe what Band Aid and Live Aid were about..
I can use evidence to talk about the importance of television.
I can look at what the campaigns achieved and decide on their importance, using evidence.

How much has Britain changed in the last century?

Objectives

By the end of this lesson you will be able to:

- explore how life changed in Britain over the 20th century
- understand why these changes have occurred

This unit has explored life in Britain since 1900. There have been big changes in nearly everything we do. In fact, some historians argue that life is changing faster now than at any time before in recorded history.

Getting you thinking

In 1900 Britain was the most powerful country in the world. The British Empire covered around a quarter of the world's surface – it was said that 'the sun never sets on the British Empire', Queen Victoria was on the throne, and the average salary was around £50 a year. Many people lived in poverty, or struggled to make ends meet. Britain had a population of around 30 million. Only men could vote – women (over 30) did not get the vote until 1918. It was 1928 before all women over 21 could vote. It was still rare to stay at school until the age of 12, and very few young people went to university. There were perhaps 200 women doctors in the whole country, and it was hard for women to enter many professions. Very few people owned their own homes; most had to rent a room or two to live in. Most homes had no hot and cold running water, and no toilets. Children shared a bed – sometimes as many as six or eight children would sleep 'top to tail' in the same bed.

A street in present-day Camden Town, London

Today Britain is part of the European Union, and no longer has an empire. It has a population of over 60 million, made up of people from all around the world. The average male salary in 2000 was £24,100, and for females around £15,100. Everyone over the age of 18 can vote – there is even talk of bringing the voting age down to 16. School is compulsory until the age of 16 and nearly half of young people go to university. In some professions – teaching is one – women greatly outnumber men. Most people own their own home, with all modern conveniences, and can take holidays every year.

There have been two major wars – war is often said to be the 'engine of change' – costing millions of lives. In 1900 the British Army was fighting the Boers over who should run the British colony of South Africa. In 2010, the army is fighting in Afghanistan. Think about all the changes brought about by war throughout the 20th century. How many can you list?

Assessment task

1   Look back at your work in lesson 5.1 and at the photograph of Lewisham High Street in 1900 (page 170). Now look at the photograph on this page. What are the biggest changes to the high street over the last 100 years or so?
2   Are these changes a cause or a consequence of the events you have studied in this unit?
3   How much change has there been, and how much has stayed the same?
4   Do you think Britain is a better place to live in now than in 1900? Explain your answer.

Check your level

I can begin to recognise and describe the nature and extent of change and continuity in Britain since 1900.

'One of the main changes in Britain over the last 100 years is … Other changes include …'

Level 5

I can begin to suggest reasons for change and continuity in Britain since 1900.

'Things have changed so much because of … and … On the other hand, some things have stayed the same. For instance … because …'

Level 6

I can analyse the nature and extent of change and continuity in Britain since 1900

'In some areas of life, for instance work, things have changed a great deal for many people. Computers, for instance, have revolutionised the way many people communicate by … For others, work has not changed so much. For example … is still pretty much the same, because … This might be because …'

Level 7

Conclusion: What was the greatest invention of the 20th century?

The Science Museum in London recently compiled a list of the ten greatest inventions that have had a major impact on the world. These were:

Newcomen's steam pump	1712
Electric telegraph	1839
Ford Model T car	1908
V2 rocket	1944
Discovery of DNA	1953
Stephenson's Rocket locomotive	1829
First X-ray machine	1896
Discovery of penicillin	1935
ACE computer	1950
Apollo spaceship's voyage to the moon	1969

What would be on your list, and why?

Getting you thinking

The historian Ian Dawson suggested a set of rules to decide if an event is or is not significant. Dawson said that for an event to be significant it needed to have:

- changed events at the time
- improved lots of people's lives – or made them worse
- changed people's ideas
- had a long lasting impact on their country or the world
- been a really good or a very bad example to other people of how to live or behave

Which of these rules applies to each of the ten inventions on the Science Museum list?

The astronaut Buzz Aldrin steps onto the surface of the moon, 1969

For example, would you argue that Ford's Model T car changed events at the time or improved lots of people's lives – or made them worse? Before World War One, most people could not afford a car, yet cars probably improved lots of people's lives, especially in rural areas. Today, however, when city streets are jammed with cars, when road traffic accidents kill and injure so many people and CO_2 emissions from cars are blamed for contributing to global warming, perhaps we might argue that cars make many – not all – people's lives worse.

Similarly, the V2 rocket in 1944 made many people's lives worse – it was used by the Nazis to bomb London and other European cities. More people died in the 1944 Blitz than in the 1940-41 bombing. Yet the V2 rocket was used to develop space travel and put a man on the moon. Perhaps today we might argue that the V2 rocket has been a force for good, rather than evil.

Significance, therefore, can vary over time. In the example above, the motor car could be very significant from 1908 to, say, the 1980s – although we might argue that it was much less significant after that. Or it might be very significant in a positive way if we talk about its role in creating jobs and wealth. If we emphasise clean energy, however, then its significance might be much more negative. It all depends on the questions you ask, and the point of view you hold.

Above: the ACE computer, 1950; a model of the DNA molecule; right: Conrad Röntgen, the discoverer of X-rays

Now it's your turn APP

1 Make a list of greatest inventions in the 20th century in each of the following categories: political; economic; social; cultural.
Try to have two or three inventions in each category.
2 Make a list of greatest inventions in the 20th century in each of the following categories: medical; consumer goods; warfare; the world of work; travel.
3 With a partner, try to decide which you think is the greatest invention of the 20th century. Explain your choice to your partner. Listen to your partner's choice. How similar are their reasons to yours?

Check your progress

I can decide on some of the greatest inventions of the 20th century.
I can decide which invention is the greatest, and give reasons.
I can think about inventions in different categories, and try to make links between them.

Conclusion: When would *you* have preferred to live?

You have studied the 20th century in this book, and should now be in a position to make up your own mind as to which was the best part of the century to live in.

Getting you thinking

This is what these students think:

I think the best time to be alive would have been before World War One. Britain ruled the world, everyone respected Britain, and came to us for help. Life was getting better – the first old age pensions were introduced – okay, it was only 5 shillings a week (25p), but it was a start. Old people could live in dignity.

You're wrong. The best time would have been the 1930s. All those new houses, new industries and new jobs. Building everywhere! Talking colour films at the cinema, like *Gone With The Wind*; and all the glamour of Hollywood. Airships and the first transatlantic flights. Frozen foods. Britain held the record for the fastest train in the world.

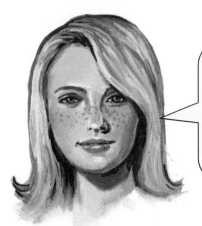

It would have been during World War Two. Of course it would be dangerous, with bombs dropping and your father away fighting, wondering if you were ever going to see him again... But at least you would be proud to be British, standing up against the Nazis, and winning. And with rationing everybody had enough to eat – fair shares for all!

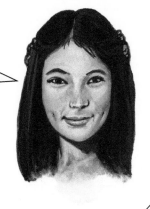

Easy – the 1960s. What a time of change! The Beatles, the miniskirt, young people led the way in fashion and spending. Don't forget those first package holidays to Spain and Greece, as well as supersonic travel in Concorde – if you could afford it – and man reaching the moon. And of course England won the World Cup!

1989. That was the year the Berlin Wall came down and the Cold War ended. No more communism, no more superpower rivalry. Tiananmen Square. The beginning of the end of apartheid in South Africa; everyone could concentrate on making money. Computers, the internet, mobile phones, satellite TV; Disneyworld opens, the first Game Boy goes on sale. What a year!

Simple! Today is the best time. I have my own room, my Wii, Nintendo DS and a DVD player. We are going to Barbados for a holiday this year, but I don't think it will be as good as Mauritius was last year! Life has never been better.

Which aspects of the century has each student focused on in making their minds up? They have each created their own *interpretation* of the century. They have weighed up the evidence and come to a conclusion about what they think is the best time to live. Do you agree with them?

Now it's your turn

1　What aspects of the period has each of the students focused on in making their interpretation? Have they used all the evidence, or only some of it?
2　Can you put together a different view of each period, using different evidence?
3　Which period would you have preferred to live in? Why?

Check your progress

★　I can talk about different interpretations of the past.
★★　I can decide on whether I agree with different interpretations, and give reasons.
★★★　I can make my own judgement on the best moment in the century to live in, and give reasons..

Conclusion: Who do you think was the most important person of the 20th century?

Time magazine, an American weekly political magazine, has chosen a 'Man of the Year' every year since 1927. Winners have included Charles Lindbergh, Mahatma Gandhi, Franklin D. Roosevelt, Adolf Hitler, Joseph Stalin, Winston Churchill, John F. Kennedy, Martin Luther King, Anwar El Sadat, Lech Walesa, Mikhail Gorbachev and Barack Obama – quite a collection!

In 1999 the magazine chose their 'Person of the Century'. They decided the most important person of the 20th century was Albert Einstein. Who would you would choose as your 'Person of the Century'?

Time magazine's 'Person of the Century', the physicist Albert Einstein (1879–1955)

Getting you thinking

You have now completed your Key Stage 3 history course, and should be in a position to make some 'big judgements' about individuals and their place in history. Why do we remember some people and not others? Why do some people remain important to us whereas others disappear from view? And do the reasons people remain important to us change over time?

Think about the Time 'Man of the Year' winners in the list above (there have been one or two women – the list was renamed 'Person of the Year'). Do you agree with the list? It may have been a surprise to find Hitler as 'Man of the Year', but perhaps it is not so surprising for the year 1938. Would he have been 'Man of the Year' in 1940 for example, or in 1944? Similarly, Winston Churchill was first named 'Man of the Year' in 1940. Would he have been in with a chance of winning the title in 1935 or 1938? Timing is everything.

You can find the full list of 'Men of the Year' on the internet at:
http://en.wikipedia.org/wiki/Time_Person_of_the_Year

Now it's your turn

1 Look at the list showing selected 'Men of the Year.' Are there any names on the list that surprise you? Are there any names that you think should not be there? Why?

2 Are there any names that, from your study of history, you think ought to be added to the list? For which year would you add them? Why?

3 What do you think should be the criteria for choosing a 'Person of the Year?'

4 Albert Einstein (1879–1955) was chosen by Time Magazine as 'Person of the Century.' He was a famous scientist who won the Nobel Prize for Physics in 1921 for his theory of relativity; he is regarded as the father of modern physics. He was German, but left Germany and went to America in 1933 when the Nazis came to power. He lived and worked there until his death. Why do you think Albert Einstein was chosen as 'Person of the Century'?

5 What criteria would you use to choose a 'Person of the Century'? Would you choose a scientist, a politician, a military leader or an inventor?

6 Make a short list of people you think ought to be considered for such a title. Work with a partner. Compare your lists, and produce a joint list. Now join with another pair of students. Again, compare lists and see if you can agree who should be 'Person of the Century.'

7 Once you have agreed, prepare a short presentation as a group, justifying your choice.

Check your progress

I can talk about some of the people chosen as 'Man of the Year'.

I can make a judgement about the significance of some of these people.

I can reach my own conclusion about who should be 'Person of the Century', and give reasons.

So, what is history?

Objectives

By the end of this lesson you will be able to:

- reflect on what you have learned in Key Stage 3 history
- give your own opinion of what is meant by history

This is your final Key Stage 3 history lesson. It is time to reflect on what you have learned, and what you now understand by the term 'history.' What will you take away from your history course? What will you remember? What do you wish you had known at the start of Year 7?

Getting you thinking

History is split into *content* – for example, 1066, Magna Carta, the Suffragettes, Empire, World War One etc; and *concepts and ideas* – for example, significance, interpretation, diversity, chronology etc. *Both* aspects of history are equally important in understanding the past. And the reason for trying to understand the past is to help us understand what has made the world we live in today the way it is.

Key concepts developed during this course

Chronological understanding
I can recognise the order in which events have happened and what it was like in different periods of history.

Significance
I can judge the significance of people and/or events, for example, was Mrs Thatcher the greatest 20th century prime minister?

Cultural, ethnic and religious diversity
I can understand that people in the past and present are all different. Medieval peasants' lives, for instance, were very different from our lives today.

Change and continuity
I can understand how much has changed between 1066 and today and how much has stayed the same.

Cause and consequence
I can explain why events in the past took place and what the results were; for example, why the English Civil War started, and the results.

Interpretations
I can look at the different opinions historians have about history; for example, whether the Industrial Revolution made life better or worse.

Important content you have learned about during this course

Norman Conquest   Getting the vote   World War One   Magna Carta

Empire   World War Two   Feudalism   The workhouse

Cold War   Dissolution of the monasteries   Slave trade   Russia

Crusades   American War of Independence   Hitler   Black Death

Decolonisation   Holocaust   English Civil War   Ireland

Afghanistan   Cholera   India   Migration

Now it's your turn   APP

You are going to produce a page for the history department website, describing your Key Stage 3 course. An effective web page will have around 200–300 words and at most a couple of images. This will involve some very careful selection.

Step 1: Are you going to focus on *content* or *concepts and ideas*? You need to decide which to give more emphasis to.

Step 2: How are you going to select the content to include – on the basis of enjoyment, interest, relevance, importance or something else?

Step 3: Which concepts are you going to emphasise? Each spread of this series has focused on helping you to develop your confidence in one of these important historical concepts. Which of these do you think is more relevant to you and your future studies?

Step 4: Is there a list of things you really feel you *have* to include, that you think it is essential to know and be able to do by the end of Key Stage 3?

Step 5: How are you going to present these in an interesting way that will capture the imagination of your intended audience – those about to start on their Key Stage 3 course – without 'telling them all the answers'?

Step 6: The easy bit! Produce your web page.

Check your level

I can suggest some things we should study in history, and explain why we should study them.

Level **5**

I can suggest both content and concepts we should study in history, and explain their significance in our study of history.

Level **6**

I can reflect meaningfully on my own learning in order to produce an effective web page for Year 7 students starting their Key Stage 3 History course, highlighting things of particular relevance to them.

Level **7**

Glossary

14 Points: set of proposals put forward by the US president as a basis for ending the war

Abdicated: stood down

Abundant: lots and lots

Aggressors: the people responsible for starting a war

Allah: Muslim term for God

Alliance: coalition of countries agreeing to work together for the same aims

Allied Naval Blockade: blocking off Germany's ports to prevent it importing food or raw materials for the war effort

Alliteration: repetition of the same consonant sound at the start of two or more words that are near each other

Allowance: regular amount

Amphibious: involving attack on both sea and land

Anti-Semitism: prejudice against Jewish people

Appalled: really upset

Archivist: someone who looks after the records

Armistice: agreement to stop fighting

Assassination: the killing of a public figure

Assisted passage: cheap fare, subsidised by the country you are going to, to encourage immigrants

Atrocities: acts of exceptional brutality and violence

Austerity: shortages of food and clothes, no luxuries, 'belt-tightening'

Ballistic missiles: missiles that are guided at start but fall freely towards their targets

Barbarously: very cruelly

Battalion: fighting unit of around 1,000 men

Benefit: regular payments by the state in times of need

Billeted: made to live with

Black Hand Gang: terrorists who wanted Bosnia to be part of Serbia

Blackshirts: uniformed members of the BUF

Blitzkrieg: literally 'lightning war', quick surprise strikes with support from warplanes

Boom: time of economic prosperity

Butler: personal servant

Bystander: someone who stands by and observes but is not involved in an event

Called up: conscripted

Capitol: where US Congress meets in Washington

Casualties: soldiers killed or wounded in battle

Cheka: the Russian secret police

Coalition government: a government made up of different parties who have agreed to cooperate

Collaborated: worked with the coalition

Collaborators: people from other nations who helped the Nazis

Collective farms: state-owned but run by the peasants

Colony: one country owned or controlled by a bigger more powerful one

Commemorating: remembering

Communism: a political system developed from Karl Marx's ideas

Commuted: changed, substituted

Compensated: given money to make up for their loss

Compulsion: being forced to do something

Concession: a right

Conflicting: contradictory, inconsistent, saying different things

Conscription: the process of making all men join the army for a set time

Consumer: someone who buys goods to use for themselves

Criteria: standards by which something can be judged

Cultural Revolution: attempt to completely change public opinion and behaviour

DCSF: UK government's Department for Culture, Media and Sport

Defendants: those charged with crimes

Demilitarised zone: An area where no German soldiers were allowed to be stationed

Demobilised: let out of the army

Demolition: being knocked down

Demoralise: destroy confidence, cause chaos

Depression: economic slump with high unemployment

Dignitary: a person of high rank or position

Disembarked: brought ashore from a ship

Dismantled: taken to pieces

Disposable wealth: money to spend on non-essential items

Dole: unemployment pay

Drudgery: boring, repetitive housework and jobs

Duma: the Russian parliament

Dustbowl: a desert-like region, where food cannot be grown

Embalmed: preserved using chemicals

Emigrate: leave your own country to go and live elsewhere

Employment vouchers: permission to work

Enigma machine: a machine used to encode and decode secret messages

Entitlement: claim

Ethnic cleansing: the violent removal of one ethnic group by another ethnic group

Executed: put to death

Exiled: forced to move away from home and friends

Feckless: wasteful, useless

Feminist movement: women trying to make their life better

Firestorm: an uncontrollable fire caused by bombing

First past the post: a system where each party fights for individual seats and the party with the most seats is given power

Franco-Prussian War: a war between France and Prussia in 1870-1871, won by Prussia

Frivolity: lighthearted enjoyment

Genocide: the killing of an entire national, racial, religious, or ethnic group

Gourmet: top quality

Great Powers: Germany, Austria-Hungary, Russia, France and Britain

Great Powers: in 1919 these were Britain, France, Germany and the USA

Guerrillas: irregular soldiers, attempting to overthrow a government

Haemophilia: a disease that prevents blood from clotting

Holocaust: a biblical word for sacrifice

Home front: the work of people at home in Britain in support of the war effort

Hypothesis: an idea of what might be true for which you need to find evidence

Iconic: very famous and significant

Ideologies: ideas or beliefs that form the basis of a political or economic system

Illegal: against the law

Incapacitate: injure but not kill

Independence: not being ruled by another country

Indispensable: absolutely necessary

Infer: make guesses based on evidence

Integrated: part of mainstream society

Intellectual: academic, person who works with their mind, thinker

Intrigued: tried to undermine or remove

Jerry-built: built as quickly and cheaply as possible

Jihad: holy war

Jihadi: active Muslim supporter of holy war

Kaiser: emperor of Germany

Kamikaze: suicide bomber

Lamentable: unfortunate, sad

LPs: long-playing records

Luftwaffe: German air force

Maimed: lost one or more of limbs

Means test: a test of income which determines who is eligible for benefits

Militia: unofficial, private army made up of civilians

Minorities: small groups within a population

Mobilise: get your armies ready for war

Mobilised: called up to fight in the armed forces

Monetarist policies: controlling the economy by limiting how much money there is available to spend

Morality: rightness, acceptability

Mujahadeen: Afghan rebels who fought the Soviets

Mutinies: soldiers and sailors refusing to obey orders

Nationalised: when factories are taken away from private owners and run by the state. The profits then belong to the state.

Nationalities: people with a common historical background and identity

Noncombatants: civilians, people who are not part of the military

North Atlantic Treaty Organisation (NATO): a Western organisation set up in 1949 to promote collective security during the Cold War

Noxious: harmful to health

Numbskull: stupid, with no skills

Over the top: leaving the British trenches to attack the German trenches

Pandemic: major outbreak of disease

Patriot: someone who is proud of their country

Pauper funeral: no coffin and no marked grave, paid for by the Poor Law

Pauper: someone with no money and no job

Pawnbroker: shopkeeper who loaned money to borrowers who had something valuable to leave as a deposit

Pentagon: USA military headquarters

Perilous: very dangerous

Perpetrator: someone who carries out an act

Persecute: victimise, harass or treat unfairly because of religion or ethnic origins

Pilfered: stole

Pillbox: concrete shelter for machine guns

Glossary

Pinned down: military term for a unit that is being suppressed by enemy fire

Plundering: wholesale theft of valuables

Political agitator: someone who stirs up public feeling about issues

Predominant: most influential

Prefabs: houses made in sections, and delivered to be erected

Prize money: share of the money from a captured ship

Product: an item made for sale

Prohibition: the banning of the production and sale of alcohol in the USA

Proletariat: the industrial working class

Propaganda: information put out by a government or other organisation to influence people's opinions

Proportional representation: a system which allocates seats in parliament based on the percentage of the vote received

Prudish: easily offended by matters relating to sex

Rearm: build weapons such as tanks and bombs

Reconciliation: being prepared to be friends with former enemies

Reconnaissance: exploring an area to gather military information

Reform: change

Renown: fame

Reparations: payments by Germany for the damaged caused in World War One

Reprisals: military action in response to an enemy's attacks

Reservist: someone who has served in the army and who will be called up again if war breaks out

Robben Island: South African penal colony for political prisoners

Sanctions: peaceful actions against a country aimed at forcing it to change

Scullion: servant doing the worst tasks in the kitchen

Settlers: people who settle in a new country or colony

Sharecropper: a farmer who rented the land he farmed by giving the landowner a share of the crop as payment

Solitary confinement: a kind of imprisonment in which the prisoner is completely alone, with no contact with other people

Speakeasies: illegal drinking clubs set up during prohibition

Squalor: dirt, filth

Squits: diarrhoea

Stalemate: neither side winning, or losing

State funeral: special funeral, organised by the government, to honour a very important person who has died

Stigma: shame

Strafing: attacking targets on the ground from low-flying aircraft

Street furniture: objects for public use – post boxes, benches etc

Strongpoint: specially strengthened defensive position

Subscription: regular weekly payment

Subsistence economy: an economy in which people grow enough food to feed only themselves

Substantiate: confirm or support an idea

Suicide bomber: someone prepared to kill themselves to injure others

Suppressed: put down, destroyed

Sympathy strike: strikes in support of other industries on strike

Synonymous: meaning the same as

Taliban: radical Islamic group

Tariffs: taxes placed on goods that are made outside the country

Tenements: low-rental apartment buildings, often of poor quality

The Balkans: part of southeast Europe

Traveller's cheques: safe form of money that can be changed into local currency anywhere in the world

Vandalism: wilful destruction of property

Verdun: major battle on the Western Front between Germany and France in June 1916

Warsaw Pact: an East European organisation set up in 1955 to promote collective security during the Cold War

Workhouse: the poor had to go into the workhouse to get help from the Poor Law authorities. Conditions were worse in the workhouse than outside

Yiddish: spoken language of Jewish people, which originated in Eastern Europe

Index

Index

Index

Acknowledgements

The publishers gratefully acknowledge the permission granted to reproduce the copyright material in this book. While every effort has been made to trace and contact copyright holders, where this has not been possible the publishers will be pleased to make the necessary arrangements at the first opportunity.

p.10 Sue Wilkinson **p.12** Illustrated London News Ltd/Mary Evans **p.14** From *Brothers In War*, (Ebury Press), provided by Michael Walsh **p.16** Sue Wilkinson **p.17** Quotation from *Battlebags: British Airships of the Great War*, by Ces Mowthorpe, Alan Sutton Publishing, 1995 **p.18** Topham Picturepoint **p.21** Getty Images **p.22** Copyright © South Western Examinations Board, 1980, quotation from *Europe's Last Summer*, by David Fromkin, Vintage, 2005 **p.24** FPG/Hulton Archive/Getty Images, quotation from *Bradlibs.com Oral Recording*, Private George Morgan, Ist Bradford Pals, interviewed in 1976, URL http://www.bradlibs.com/bradford/book/chapter%203%20(37-61).pdf, accessed 01/03/2010 **p.26** Getty Images **p.28** Getty Images **p.29** Source 2 quotation from *Cannon Fodder: An Infantryman's Life on the Western Front, 1914-18*, by A. Stuart Dolden, Blandford Press, 1980, source 3 quotation of Private Harold Horne, from *Tommy Goes to War*, by Malcolm Brown, Dent & Sons, 1978. Reprinted by permission from The History Press, source 4 quotation from *The Long Carry: the Journal of Stretcher Bearer Frank Dunham, 1916-18*, by Frank Dunham, Pergamon, 1970, source 5 quotation from *The Great War*, by Correlli Barnett, BBC Books, 2003. Reprinted with permission of David Higham Associates **p.31** Topham Picturepoint **p.32** The Granger Collection/TopFoto **p.34** Courtesy of The British Postal Museum & Archive **p.35** Quotation from 'Women at War', by Peter Craddick-Adams, *Wars & Conflicts, BBC History Website*, URL http://www.bbc.co.uk/history/trail/wars_conflict/home_front/ women_at_war_10.shtml, accessed 01/03/2010 **p.36** Quotation from *Sapper Martin: The Secret Great War Diary of Jack Martin*, edited by Richard Van Emden, Bloomsbury, 2009 **p.37** The Granger Collection/TopFoto **p.38** Popperfoto/Getty Images **p.39** Source 1 quotation from Charles Hudson, from *Soldier, Poet, Rebel*, by Miles Hudson, The History Press, 2007, source 2 quotation from *War Memoirs of David Lloyd George*, by David Lloyd George, Odhams Press, 1933, source 3 quotation from 'Historic Figures', URL http://www.bbc.co.uk/history/historic_figures/haig_douglas_ general.shtml, accessed 01/03/2010 **p.40** Popperfoto/Getty Images **p.42** World History Archive/TopFoto **p.43** Shutterstock, quotation from *Hulton New Histories: 5 Peace and War*, Philip A Sauvain, Hulton Educational Publications, 1985 **p.45** Quotation from *With a Machine-gun to Cambrai*, George Coppard, Cassell Military Paperbacks, Orion Publishing, 1969 **p.48** Time & Life Pictures/Getty Images **p.50** TopFoto **p.53** TopFoto **p.54** National Motor Museum/HIP/TopFoto **p.56** The Granger Collection/TopFoto **p.58** Source 1 quotation from *The New Negro, An Interpretation, by Alain Locke*, Albert and Charles Boni, 1925, source 2 quotation from *The Collected Works of Langston Hughes*, by Langston Hughes, Arnold Rampersad, Joseph McLaren. Reprinted with permission of David Higham Associates **p.59** The Granger Collection/TopFoto, quotation from November issue of *The Crisis*, by Ella Baker and Marvel Cooke, The Crisis Publishing Company Inc, 1935 **p.60** TopFoto **p.62** *Brother, Can You Spare a Dime?* lyrics by E.Y. Harburg, Music by Jay Gorney. Copyright © 1932 (renewed) WB Music Corp. (ASCAP). Copyright © Carlin Music **p.63** TopFoto **p.65** The Granger Collection/TopFoto **p.66** The Art Archive/Bibliothèque des Arts Décoratifs Paris/Gianni Dagli Orti **p.69** World History Archive/TopFoto **p.70** The Art Archive/Private Collection/Marc Charmet **p.71** Quotation from *The Romanovs: the Final Chapter*, by Robert K. Massie, Arrow Book, 1995. Reprinted by permission of the Random House Group LTD **p.72** The Art Archive/Eileen Tweedy **p.73** Quotation from *Mein Kampf*, by Adolf Hitler, Pimlico, 1992 **p.74** World History Archive/TopFoto **p.75** Quotation from *The Guardian*, 8 June 1934. Reprinted by permission of *the Guardian* **p.76** Popperfoto/Getty Images **p.77** Source 1-3 from *Survival: Holocaust Survivors Tell Their Story*, edited by Wendy Whitworth, Quill Press, 2003, source 4 from *The Diary of a Young Girl: The definitive edition by Anne Frank*, edited by Susan Massotty, Viking, 1997. Copyright © The Anne Frank-Fonds, Basle, Switzerland, 1991 **p.78** Getty Images **p.79** Source 1 quotation from *I Came Alone: The Stories of the Kindertransports*, edited by Bertha Leverton and Samuel Lowensohn, Book Guild, 1990, source 2 quotation from the *Kindertransport*, by Diane Samuels, Nick Hern Books, 1995. Copyright © Diane Samuels 1995 **p.82** Roger-Viollet/TopFoto **p.84** Quotation from 'Aboard the U.S.S. Oahu at Shanghai' 17 December 1937, *The New York Times*. Reprinted with permission of the New York Times, PARS International **p.85** Imagno/Austrian Archives/TopFoto, quotation from *They Were in Nanjing: The Nanjing Massacre Witnessed by American and British Nationals*, by Suping Lu, Hong Kong University Press, 2004 **p.87** Evening Standard, with permission from Solo Syndication **p.88** Artmedia/HIP/TopFoto **p.89** Source 1 quotation from *For Whom the Bell Tolls by Ernest Hemingway*, published by Jonathan Cape. Reprinted by permission of The Random House Group Ltd, source 2 quotation from *A Moment of War*, by Laurie Lee, Penguin Books, 1991. Copyright © Laurie Lee, 1991 **p.90** Shutterstock **p.91** The Granger Collection/TopFoto, Topham Picturepoint/TopFoto **p.92** Topham Picturepoint **p.96** British Cartoon Archive, University of Kent **p.99** Copyright © Rand McNally **p.100** TopFoto **p.101** Quotation of Angela Sexton, quoted in *The Home Front in Britain, 1939-1945*, by Alastair and Anne Pike, Tressell Publications, 1985 **p.102** TopFoto **p.103** TopFoto **p.104** Topham Picturepoint/TopFoto **p.105** Topham Picturepoint **p.108** Source A TopFoto, source B Topham Picturepoint, source C Public Record Office/HIP, source D Granger Collection/TopFoto, source D Imperial War Museum, source E Imperial War Museum **p.110** David Martin **p.111** Leamington Spa **p.112** The Granger Collection/TopFoto **p.113** Quotation from *Dresden: Tuesday 13 February 1945*, by Frederick Taylor, Bloomsbury Publishing, 2004. Reprinted with permission of Bloomsbury Publishing **p.115** Topham Picturepoint/TopFoto **p.116** Getty Images **p.118** TopFoto/Caro **p.120** Source 1 RIA Novosti/TopFoto, source 2 Roger-Viollet/TopFoto **p.121** Getty Images **p.122** Print Collector/HIP/TopFoto **p.124** DreamWorks/Everett/Rex Features **p.125** Everett Collections/Rex Features, quotation from D-Day, June 6, 1944: The Climactic Battle of World War II, by Stephen Ambrose, Simon & Schuster, 2002 **p.126** TopFoto, extracts from the Amazon.co.uk website review **p.127** Quotation from *History Alive 4*, by Peter Moss, Hart Davis Educational, 1977 **p.128** American Photographer, (20th century)/Private Collection/The Bridgeman Art Library, quotation from *Full Hearts and Empty Bellies*, by Winifred Foley, Abacus, 2009 **p.129** Quotation from Life in Britain since 1700, by Peter and Mary Speed, OUP, 1982. Copyright © Peter and Mary Speed 1982. Reprinted by permission of Oxford University Press **p.130** The Granger Collection/TopFoto, quotation reprinted with the permission of the Quinton Local History Society **p.131** Quotation reprinted with permission from Black Country Living Museum **p.132** Getty Images, quotation from the book review by Piers Brendon, reviewing *'We Danced All Night': A Social History of Britain Between the Wars,'* by Martin Pugh, The Guardian, 5 July 2008. Reprinted by permission of *the Guardian* **p.133** Quotation from *From Workhouse to Welfare: The development of the Welfare State*, by Ian Martin, Penguin Education, 1971 **p.134** Quotation from 'Safe as Prefabs – Grade II Listing Preserves Second World War Relics', by Peter Walker, *The Guardian*, 17 March 2009. Reprinted by permission of *the Guardian* **p.135** Table from *An Introduction to Modern British History 1900-1999*, by Michael Lynch, Hodder & Stoughton, 2001 **p.138** Shutterstock **p.141** Reprinted with permission from USS Ronald Reagan Publicity Office **p.143** Getty Images **p.144** RIA Novosti/TopFoto **p.150** Ullstein Bild/TopFoto **p.153** Time & Life Pictures/Getty Images **p.156** Aurora Photos **p.158** Andrew Wrenn **p.161** TopFoto/ImageWorks **p.162** Collection International Institute of Social History, Amsterdam **p.163** Shutterstock **p.164** Getty Images **p.166** Source 1 TopFoto/EMPICS, source 2 Warner BR/Everett/Rex Features **p.168** Reprinted with permission from USS Ronald Reagan Publicity Office **p.170** London Stereoscopic Company/Getty Images **p.172** Source 1 Alf Wilkinson, source 2 Alf Wilkinson **p.173** National Archives **p.176** The Granger Collection/TopFoto **p.178** Popperfoto/Getty Images **p.179** Little, Brown Book Group **p.180** SSPL via Getty Images **p.182** Beamish Open Air Museum, Durham **p.184** Hulton Archive/Getty Images **p.186** Getty Images Herbert Felton/Herbert Felton/Getty Images **p.188** Alf Wilkinson **p.190** Topham Picturepoint/TopFoto **p.193** SSPL via Getty Images **p.195** SSPL via Getty Images **p.196** Punch Limited/TopFoto **p.198** Courtesy of The Advertising Archives **p.200** David Gamble/TopFoto **p.202** Getty Images **p.204** Redferns **p.206** Shutterstock **p.208** The Granger Collection/TopFoto **p.209** TopFoto/National **p.209** Topham Picturepoint **p.210** Print Collector/HIP/TopFoto **p.212** Getty Images